DAMNED IF YOU DO, DAMNED IF YOU DON'T

For Ernie Gullerud

Damned if you do,
Damned if you don't
Working in child welfare

ANTHONY McMAHON

Ashgate

Aldershot · Brookfield USA · Singapore · Sydney

Published by
Ashgate Publishing Ltd
Gower House
Croft Road
Aldershot
Hants GU11 3HR
England

Ashgate Publishing Company
Old Post Road
Brookfield
Vermont 05036
USA

British Library Cataloguing in Publication Data

McMahon, Anthony
    Damned if you do, damned if you don't : working in child
    welfare
    1. Social work with children 2. Social workers
    I. Title
    362.7 ' 6

Library of Congress Catalog Card Number: 97-74453

ISBN 1 85972 616 X

Printed and bound by Athenaeum Press, Ltd.,
Gateshead, Tyne & Wear.

Contents

Acknowledgments

This book is based on the courage and candour of the workers at City Office. They allowed me to enter their working lives at a time of great organizational and personal stress. I am grateful to them for that and for their generosity and openness in showing me what they do and why they do it. I thank them as I do the Illinois Department of Children and Family Services for allowing me to undertake this project. I hope that my regard for them and the importance of their work is evident even as I critique the circumstances in which they do their work.

There are others I must thank for their support and professional insight. I thank Ernest Gullerud, Paula Allen-Meares, and Norman Denzin for their guidance during the research and writing of this project. I would particularly like to state how much I valued Dr Gullerud's care, advice, and wisdom which he shared with me over innumerable cups of coffee. I am grateful to Golie Jansen, Sue McGinty and Alan Peshkin who gave me of their time and wisdom so that I could sharpen my skills and my perceptions.

I could not have completed this project without the critical support, insight, and experience of Suzanne McGinty. I thank her for the hours she listened to my meanderings, the many drafts of my writings she read, and the times she put up with and understood my frustrations and my elations.

Preface

This book is a study of a group of public agency child welfare workers. It records their work with abused and neglected children and their families. Child welfare work is one of the most contested arenas of social work practice. It is a form of work that society sees as necessary while, at the same time, it condemns it as intrusive interference into family life. As well, the workers' ideal of protecting children from abusive families and situations is frustrated by high case loads, excessive paperwork, personal danger, unsympathetic courts and an ideology of child protection that is inherently counterproductive. These ambiguities are summed up in the title of the book, 'Damned if you do, damned if you don't.'

1 Child welfare practice

During the final stages of the research that forms the basis for this book, child abuse became a national talking point in the United States when the image of the abused child blended biography and art. Woody Allen, a famous movie director and actor, was accused of molesting his seven year old daughter after being discovered in an affair with his former lover's daughter that had some parallels to his movie 'Husbands and Wives' (Gliatto, Huzinec, Lynn, and Johnson, 1992). As well, the major US television networks simulcast a documentary on victims and perpetrators of child abuse. The simulcast's host, talkshow star Oprah Winfrey, introduced the documentary by relating her own story of abuse which began with her rape when she was nine years old (Levitt, Mills, and Freedman, 1992). Finally, the symbol of the abused child became a metaphor for wasted lives when sportswriters accused the US women's gymnastic team of child abuse after the failure of Olympic athletes in Barcelona, Spain (Press, 1992). These high profile examples are in sharp contrast to the mundane horror of day-to-day child abuse and neglect. These cases, a young boy tortured with burning cigarettes by his mother's boyfriend, a baby girl left alone in a car while her mother drinks in a bar, a young girl raped by her stepfather while her mother is at work, remain hidden, known only to a few. They only come to public attention if the incidents are particularly gruesome or titillating.

In the United States, as in other countries, public child welfare agencies are mandated to receive, investigate, and act on reports of abuse or neglect of a child (Kinard, 1987). Agencies provide residual services for children whose parents have somehow 'failed' them (Kadushin, 1987). Public child welfare work involves a dual, even ambiguous, role. It comprises an investigative, coercive, child removing dimension and a helping, supportive, family preserving dimension (Pelton, 1989). What connects

1

each of these stories is the urge, the necessity, to protect children who are incapable – too young, too weak, too vulnerable – of protecting themselves. The practice of child welfare touches the lives of literally hundreds of thousands of American children and their families, so the study of what workers do and what they understand of what they do is an important question.

This research project is about workers mandated by the state to protect tortured, neglected, and abused children, like those described above, when their plight is made public. How do child welfare workers go about their work? How do they describe what they do? How do they understand the experience of doing child welfare work? This study explores the lived experience of one group of eight workers whom I asked to become aware of and reflect on their working lives and experience. Drawing on Dilthey, Merleau-Ponty and Gadamer, van Manen describes lived experience as the immediate, aware consciousness of living. It is an interpretive reflection on past experience (van Manen, 1990). In the course of this research, I spoke to child welfare workers in their offices and joined in their conversations. I met their colleagues and their supervisors. I went with workers to visit children and to interview the children's parents. I sat on the benches at the back of Juvenile Court while judges and attorneys deliberated and decided what would become of children and what parents had to do to get their children back. I stood beside the workers while they discussed and negotiated their cases with attorneys.

This interest in how workers understand and experience child welfare practice comes from my own work experience. As a welfare officer for the West Australian Department for Community Services (WADCS), I spent six years working with Aboriginal communities in the remote north-west of Australia. As child welfare workers, one of our many responsibilities, we confronted social, physical, and personal conditions that were detrimental to Aboriginal children. Yet, rarely did we remove children from their families for their own protection. Instead, we worked with the children's families and communities to ameliorate the stressful or abusive conditions and created local solutions suitable to local needs (McMahon, 1990; McMahon and Kogolo, 1988). These solutions ranged from the establishment of schools and business enterprises to the development of culturally appropriate child protection, child welfare and child care schemes. This work required a cooperation with local Aboriginal people in accordance with the languages and the customs of that part of Aboriginal Australia. I was fortunate, too, in that I was able to join in working with colleagues, both Aboriginal and non-Aboriginal, who valued the local people's knowledge as much as they did their own (Tomlinson, 1985). The people's local knowledge (Foucault, 1980) complemented our expert knowledge. Their lived experience and local knowledge became resources and guides for practice (Weick, 1992).

Staff in other WADCS offices, faced with the same working contexts we were, acted differently. Neglected Aboriginal children were taken from their parents, delinquents were removed to city prisons, children wanting education were sent to far away dormitories. It seemed that the dissimilar experiences the children suffered originated in the dissimilar assumptions, beliefs and behaviours of the welfare officers concerned, not in the personal conditions of the children. Our practice valued local knowledge and a collaboration with communities, families and individuals who were simultaneously clients and colleagues. Other workers discounted local knowledge, reproducing the privileged monopoly of expert knowledge (Weick, 1992) and the old and familiar story of the continued removal of Aboriginal children from their families.

My own biography, therefore, shaped my interest in how child welfare workers understand and articulate their practice. In fact, I originally intended to focus more broadly on the practice of child welfare workers with Native Americans as a parallel field of practice to my own experience, but the focus of the research was further shaped by the experience of doing the research. The stresses and strains on workers, which I set out in Chapters 5, 6 and 7 and my interaction with the workers during the period of research, were so forceful that they lead me to focus my research more explicitly on the workers and their experiences. However, my interest in Native American child welfare remained and I have chosen mainly Indian cases to recreate examples of practice. This refining of the research question is typical of qualitative research and strengthens the value of my interpretation as emerging from the research site (Lincoln and Guba, 1985).

There are further reasons for undertaking a study of child welfare workers. First, and this is important for myself as a social worker and former child welfare worker, child welfare is one of the oldest fields of practice in social work (Siu and Hogan, 1989a). Second, child welfare workers are charged with primary responsibility for one of the most sensitive and stressful areas of human service delivery (Fryer, Poland, Bross, and Krugman, 1988). The importance of child welfare work is highlighted by the realisation that abuse and neglect can be devastating to an individual child and can have serious effects on a child for the rest of her/his life. Third, this importance is amplified by the enormous number of children identified as abused and neglected. There were 2.4 million reports of child maltreatment in the USA in 1990 (J. Anderson, 1990). These reports resulted in 360,000 children being in foster care in June, 1990 (Hardin, 1990) and Kantrowitz, McCormick and Wingert (1991) predicted that there might be as many as 500,000 children in care by 1995. Fourth, not only are there more children entering care but the children currently entering care have

3

more severe personal or family problems than in the past (Stein, 1987). New social problems such as cocaine- and crack-addicted babies, HIV-positive babies, and homelessness among families with children are straining the limits of the child welfare system (Kamerman and Kahn, 1990). Fifth, these new social problems may explain some of the reasons children are entering foster care at a younger age than they have in the past (J. Anderson, 1990). Sixth, despite the growing importance of child welfare work and social work's historic identification with this field of practice, not many US social workers currently work in child welfare (Hegar and Hunzeker, 1988; Kadushin, 1987). Finally, and the importance of this reason has been explained above, research and commentary that show that Native American children nationally are over-represented in the foster care population (Unger, 1977; Plantz, Hubbell, Barrett, and Dobrec, 1988) also prompted me to ask questions about child welfare workers and the way they go about their work. This question is especially relevant for a study of public agency workers since over half (52%) the Indian children in care are in public agency care and Indian children in public care are unlikely to be in Indian foster homes (Plantz *et al.*, 1988).

Research site

Denzin (1989a) defines sampling as following a set of rules that place the observer in a situation to record or elicit a set of behaviours which have some relevance for the research question. When considering a site to undertake research I was drawn to the Illinois Department of Children and Family Services (DCFS) because, as a public child welfare agency, it resembled the department I had worked for. Illinois DCFS, at that time, had 3,200 staff (Corrections, 1991) working in 80 offices throughout Illinois (Illinois Department of Children and Family Services, 1989).

Because of my original interest in child welfare practice with Native Americans, I sought a research site where DCFS was serving a Native American population. (In this book, the terms 'Native American' and 'Indian' are used interchangeably. Indian clients are identified by the name of their tribe). At the 1990 Census, there were 21,836 Native Americans in Illinois, of whom 10,289 lived in Cook County, the geographical area that is Chicago and its neighbourhoods (Bureau of the Census, 1991). For Native Americans, the Indian Child Welfare Act of 1978 (ICWA) was an attempt to regain control of Indian children after a 500 year history of destruction, exclusion, and assimilation and its impact on tribal and family life (Gullerud and McMahon, 1992). ICWA developed in response to deep concern by Native American tribes and families about the removal of large numbers of their children – seen as the destruction of Indian families

(Unger, 1977) – by child welfare authorities and their placement in non-Indian foster homes, adoptive homes and institutions. Despite ICWA, however, the high rate at which Native American children enter the child welfare system continues. Plantz, Hubbell, Barrett and Dobrec (1988) found that the numbers of Indian children in care increased 25% between 1980 and 1986 and that Native American children were 3.6 times more likely to enter substitute care than the children of the general population. I chose City Office (pseudonym) in Chicago, Illinois, as the site for my research because DCFS administrators advised me that City Office was one of the main DCFS offices in Illinois serving Native American clients.

Cook County DCFS was divided into four geographical areas, north, south, east, and west that covered the city of Chicago. At December 31, 1991, 70% of children placed in foster care in Illinois were from Cook County (Illinois Department of Children and Family Services, 1992). City Office was a former rooming house located near downtown Chicago. About 60 DCFS personnel worked from this office. Taina Aponte grew up in this neighbourhood and worked at City Office as a follow-up worker. She described the area, 'I came to this area in 1965 when I was about six years old. This neighbourhood was a Polish/Romanian neighbourhood. There was probably only four Latino families, Puerto Rican families. Now we have Mexican families' (Aponte, 28 May 1992). The neighbourhood has changed since she was a child, 'a time when kids could actually go out and play and not worry about strangers or being abducted or being killed or being harassed by gangs or being recruited … (now) there's a lot of drive-by shootings and gangs are not particular. If you're in the way they are going to shoot anyway. A lot of kids have been killed as a result of that.'

During the period of the fieldwork for this research, the neighbourhood was mainly African American with some Polish and Hispanic families still living in the neighbourhood. The littered streets around City Office usually held crowds of simply dressed shoppers seeking discounts in clothing and shoe shops. Near City Office, there was a children's playground with climbing frame and broken swings. The mid-morning sun reflected cheerily off the thousands of pieces of shattered glass in the sand and surrounding grass. Inside City Office, a long narrow building in red brick, workers' offices were stark and functional. Seven teams of workers with their ancillary staffs work in what were once bedrooms or lounge rooms; the closets held manuals, files and telephone directories.

Each of the three floors of City Office had a narrow corridor running the length of the building. Pinned and stuck along the walls of the corridor were posters, slogans, and notices. On the third floor, for example, AIDS and its effects on children were a prominent theme. So, too, were posters in English and Spanish warning about protection from AIDS. In one poster, a well-groomed African-American woman looked frankly out at the reader while the caption asked, 'What have you got against a condom?' The ever present background sounds were the noise of echoing, muffled voices, phones ringing in empty offices, filing cabinets trundling out and slamming shut. Outside traffic, and a passing train, were dimly heard; so too, the occasional wail of a police siren.

Marsha Williams, an African American woman in her 50s, said that each DCFS office has an atmosphere about it and that City Office was Hispanic (Field notes, 27 April 1992). The Hispanic atmosphere was more than the posters in Spanish outlining the aims and values of the Department; other DCFS offices had those. The Spanish atmosphere of this office was emphasised in the presence of many Spanish speaking workers, from Mexico, Cuba, Puerto Rico, Colombia, and the United States who worked there. Their presence was emphasised by grammatical corrections to Spanish language posters and even to the DCFS sign on the front door.

Child protection in Illinois is allegation based. David Casey, one of the child welfare workers in this study, stated that the reasons children come into care are 'physical abuse, sexual abuse and family dysfunction, a lot of times related to drug and alcohol abuse. I'd say those three main areas account for about 90% of the cases.' Family dysfunction exists in 'cases where the family hasn't physically or sexually abused the children but their basic needs aren't being met by the family because of problems; that's what we'd consider neglect' (Casey, 22 November 1991). Protective services were begun when the 24-hour Hotline at the State Central Register received a report of alleged abuse or neglect. The Hotline received over a thousand calls a day (Illinois Department of Children and Family Services, 1989). Within 24 hours each report is investigated and a judgement is made by an investigator to determine whether there is credible evidence of child abuse or neglect. When this credible evidence exists, the Department provides services to the children and their family through follow-up workers. In having an allegation based system of child protection, Illinois DCFS favours the protection of children, and their removal from their families, over prevention of situations that contribute to child abuse and neglect. This approach is typical of US child welfare programs, whether public or private, which focus on after-the-fact services emphasising child removal (Massat, 1992). (How pervasive and 'natural' child removal is was borne out one day as I was taking the bus back to the youth hostel where I stayed while doing my research. As the bus passed through one of the most notorious public housing projects in Chicago, I noticed a poster advertising Catholic Charities' foster services. The poster was of a young, White urchin and his older sister leaning out the window of an older model car. The caption read, 'David needs a place to cuddle up. Room to play, space to grow. Unfortunately, his brothers and sisters live in the car, too.' Underneath was written, 'Be a foster parent.' Removing these children from their parents and fostering them out was the only solution proposed).

In Chicago, Illinois, there are three types of child welfare workers, investigators, follow-up workers, and adoption workers, each of whom deal with differing aspects of a child welfare case. A child becomes a case in the following manner. Once a report of abuse or neglect is made it is investigated to make a determination on whether the report can be substantiated (Kinard, 1987). If the report is 'indicated' (when there is credible evidence that abuse or neglect has occurred) by an investigator, plans for further intervention and services, such as foster care, are made by a different set of workers who 'follow-up' the new case. Finally, if it is decided that the child cannot or should not be returned home, the case is transferred to a third set of workers to arrange for the child's adoption. Part of the reason for choosing one particular variant of child welfare practice – the perspective of the child welfare workers – is derived from what (Geertz, 1976, p. 223) calls 'experience-near' and 'experience-distant' concepts. An experience-near concept is one which an insider might naturally use to define what he/she sees, feels, thinks, imagines, and which is readily understood when similarly applied to others. An experience-distant concept is one which outside specialists employ to forward their scientific, philosophical, or practical aims. In research, one point of view is not to be preferred over the other.

In talking with American child welfare workers, although I was definitely an outsider, my point of nearness was my own work experience. This nearness gave me a certain knowledge of what the workers did. But because of my own training as a social worker it did more than that. In regard to craft skills, Sands (1990) has asserted that social workers are well prepared to conduct ethnographic research because direct practice resembles, in some way, ethnography. As well, Rubin (1981) has lauded the utility of clinical training for interviewing. There is no doubt that the use of everyday social work skills such as attentive listening, rapport-building, and allowing the other person to articulate their concerns, are necessary skills for the ethnographer to have.

It is in this sense of knowledge that is antecedent to the research experience that Eisner (1991) wrote of the art of appreciation, or connoisseurship, involved in research. Social work connoisseurship, involving the knowledge of theories, behaviours and values germane to social work practice, provides a ready-made context that shapes and refines perception and interpretation. At the same time, the order that connoisseurship provides can stifle and confine as well as discriminate. Eisner also wrote of the liability of antecedent knowledge – 'a way of seeing is also a way of not seeing' (Eisner, 1991, p. 67). Since this is so, there are standard procedures to develop trustworthiness in naturalistic inquiry and these procedures are discussed in the Appendix.

Doing the research

This project accords with Fanshel's (1980) valuing of research that focuses on the transactions between practitioners, clients, and social institutions and addresses Wood's (1978) concern that social work research on practice focus on process as well as on outcome. The location of the research is the interaction of the DCFS worker, other professional workers, and mainly Indian children and families among the private troubles and public issues of everyday life. Workers and clients came to this encounter with histories and social constructions of their individuality that encompass more than their own personal experiences. So, too, have I, and my history is important for this project since the doing of naturalistic inquiry values the researcher as research instrument (Lincoln and Guba, 1985). In fact, in an interpretive discourse that values the personal, the account of method must enunciate the social and ideological context (Ulmer, 1989) of the researcher. As Feyerabend has noted, scientists' rules for interpretation 'depend for their practical meaning on the variable skills, intuitions, customary knowledge, social experience and technical equipment' (1975, p. 55) of the researcher. I have already shown how my previous experiences have directed and structured my choice of topic.

After some preliminary visits, I began regularly visiting City Office in March, 1991 and completed the research at the beginning of July, 1992. The eight child welfare workers who are the focus of this study comprised all the follow-up workers at City Office who had Indian cases during the latter phase of the research. In order to understand and interpret the lived experience of the child welfare workers, I chose research methods – participant observation, interviewing, and document analysis (Denzin, 1989b) – that would allow me to bring my interpretation of the workers' experiences to the reader. The names of all workers and clients in this study have been changed to protect confidentiality as has the name and some physical details of City Office.

This study took place at a time when the Illinois DCFS was attempting reform after settling a series of lawsuits that had charged it with not doing what it was supposed to do, protect children. The then current state of Illinois DCFS was well illustrated by newspaper reports surrounding the resignation of the Director in August, 1992. These reports stated the Department was 'overworked, underfunded... a bureaucratic maze... an impossible job' (Wills, 1992). This state was not atypical; critics of the child welfare system, such as Pelton (1990), described public child welfare across

8

the US as being in a state of chaos. A report in *The New York Times* , for example, described child welfare services in New York as a system in crisis (Dugger, 1992). As a researcher, this turmoil was useful in highlighting the way child welfare was performed. Satyamurti (1981) has noted that research in times of change brings to the fore understandings that may otherwise remain unnoticed. While this turmoil may have added to my bleak portrayal of child welfare work, it did serve to illustrate clearly the characteristic dilemmas and contradictions of child welfare practice.

The turmoil in DCFS in 1992 stemmed from eight class action lawsuits alleging widespread deficiencies and discrimination against poor and Hispanic families. The settling of these lawsuits during 1991 precipitated DCFS into what it called the most far-reaching change in its history (Illinois Department of Children and Family Services, 1992). Further criticism of DCFS came from the Chicago press. Over the 16 months of my research, there was a constant dribble of largely negative media reports that criticised the Department itself or castigated individual workers. Headlines ranged from 'Tot's death triggers probe of DCFS' (Copeland, 1991) to 'Months after kids' deaths, DCFS caseworker reports they're fine' (Karwath, 1991a) to 'DCFS fires caseworker paid to stay at home' (Karwath, 1991b). The most celebrated and sustained campaign was that by columnist Bob Greene (1990) and journalist Rob Karwath (1991c) who, from March 1990 to late 1991 chronicled the case of Baby 'Sarah,' a DCFS foster child returned to her natural mother against the foster parents' wishes. According to the workers I interviewed, this negative attention devalued the work they did and negatively influenced Juvenile Court staff towards them. Stehno (1990, p. 559) considered 'relentlessly critical Monday morning quarterbacks (found most frequently in press rooms and legal advocates' offices)' as a major obstacle to public support of child welfare workers in Illinois.

Theoretical contexts

Research methods are only of use when judged in the light of the theoretical perspectives in which they are used (Denzin, 1989b). My purpose in this research was to see, describe and understand the social interactions of people engaging in action (Blumer, 1986). For this project, social interaction means what workers, clients, and other interested parties do together and what workers talk and write about to define their social encounters. Following Blumer (1986), I see meaning arising from the process of interaction between people: meanings are social products. So, too, is the language the child welfare workers use to talk and write about their clients. In acting and speaking people show who they are; their identity is implicit in what they say and do (Arendt, 1958). Imre (1991,

9

p. 198) has noted that, 'words incorporate beliefs, and there is increasing awareness that beliefs underlie all knowledge and ways of viewing the world.' We do this even if we cannot articulate that vision clearly; there is no position that is atheoretical (Horkheimer, 1989).

My concern, however, is not just with personal meanings. I seek to contextualise those meanings within the wider historical and political context of child welfare practice. In this, I have followed Denzin's (1989a) continuation of C. Wright Mills' project of connecting personal troubles, such as abuse and neglect, with public policies and institutions that have been created to address those personal problems (Mills, 1959). Denzin's approach, which he has called interpretive interactionism, 'attempts to make the world of lived experience directly accessible to the reader. It endeavours to capture the voices, emotions, and actions of those studied' (1989a, p. 10). Allied with an interpretive interactionist approach, I drew on ethno-methodological studies of 'naturally occurring mundane occasions' (Atkinson, 1988, p. 442) which portrayed everyday life and interaction in settings such as child welfare agencies (Pithouse, 1987) and law courts (Maynard, 1984; Pollner, 1987). Ethnomethodology, based on the work of Garfinkel (1967), has contributed to our understanding of the social production of 'facts' in written and spoken accounts of diagnoses and assessments. Ethnomethodology reveals 'the richly layered skills, assumptions and practices through which the most commonplace (and not so commonplace) activities and experiences are constructed' (Pollner, 1987, p. ix). In doing this, it acts as a critical counter to the interactionists' perceived lack of analysis of the actor's point of view (Silverman, 1985). It is particularly useful for setting out the everyday work practices that workers take for granted.

A further theoretical stance from which I conducted my research is drawn from social work. Witkin and Gottschalk (1988) have called for social work research that explicates the underlying assumptions of actions and the social meanings they signify. For them, because social science is infused with moral and political assumptions, social critique and a concern for social justice are necessary reflections of social work values. For many social workers, social injustice, lack of political participation, and domination give rise to the social conditions that produce their clients (Burghardt, 1986; Findlay, 1978; Leonard, 1984). I, too, came to this project with a critical theory of society which understands and contextualises injustice within its social, political and historical world (Kellner, 1989). My research, then, is critical research (Denzin, 1989b).

In proposing critical research I have taken account of the criticisms of ethnography that fault its pretensions to a naturalistic realism (Denzin, 1989b; Marcus and Fischer, 1986; Thomas, 1983). The urban ethnography of the Chicago School and anthropological writings of the past have tended to value dominant class and colonialist social values over those of 'deviant' groups or 'primitive' peoples. Thus, for Thomas (1983) the writers of the Chicago School, in their pursuit of naturalism, operated from a medical model of society that pathologised Chicago's underclasses. Their studies of the 'underdog' – hobos, petty criminals, gangs, waitresses, dance hall musicians – supplied valuable ethnographic detail but were partial (Silverman, 1985) and apolitical (Thomas, 1983). In contrast, I reach back to the older social work tradition of social surveys that originated at the beginning of the twentieth century. The research of LePlay in France, of Charles Booth, Mayhew, and the Webbs in England, and of settlement workers like Jane Addams in Chicago critiqued the social problems of their day and sought social change through reform (Bogdan and Biklen, 1982).

There is value for social work in undertaking this type of research. Geertz (1973) has emphatically asserted that if you want to understand what a science is 'you should look at what the practitioners of it do' (p. 5). My research has focused on what child welfare workers do and what they say about what they do. Rein and White (1981) have noted that much of the knowledge that determines social work practice today originates in the context of practice itself. They go on to say that much of this knowledge is unrealised and unarticulated. For them, social work context implied not only the social worker's relationship with the client but the range of agencies, government structures and pressure groups that act on the worker in the agency. The social work value of this project is that it sets out to systematically reconstruct the intuitive knowledge (Habermas, 1979) of child welfare workers. It is similar to three English studies (Corby, 1987; Dingwall, Eekelaar and Murray, 1983; Pithouse, 1987) which give readers a sense of the action (Johnson, 1975) taking place in public child welfare agencies by going to the places where social workers actually work. As Scott (1990) has noted, such ethnographic description more easily conveys and makes understandable the practice wisdom of social workers.

Organisation of the book

The aim of this book is to capture the daily work experiences of child welfare workers in an inner city office in Chicago Illinois. Thus, the research on which this book is based is located in the United States context. However, the articulation of these workers' experiences will resonate with many workers around the US and in other countries. The book, however, is not an uncritical paean: their work and their description of what they do is not unquestioned. Chapter 2, for example, presents a critical, genealogical reading of child welfare ideologies and values where the historical forces that have shaped contemporary public child welfare institutions are outlined. Chapter 3 introduces the eight workers. I interpret the meanings their own biography has for them as child welfare workers. I further placed them, through their biographies, within current child welfare practice, as heirs to the second child-saving movement with its emphasis on the rescue and protection of neglected and abused children. I also introduce the Native American children and families who are part of the caseloads of the workers. In Chapter 4, after workers tell of their triumphs in protecting children and give a brief outline of a 'typical' day's work, the neat identification of workers' biographies and child welfare history begins to unravel as the workers speak about the counterproductive effects of their practice on many of the children. The realisation of the harm done to children while protecting them challenged workers' understanding of their protective mission. Chapter 5 discusses how workers attempt to form parents into passive and acquiescent clients as a precondition for having their children returned. Clients' resistance of attempts to redefine them as abusing parents further challenged workers' perceptions of themselves as child protectors. A central theme of this chapter is the impetus to bureaucratise individual clients into an homogenous general client for the purpose of paperwork documentation.

Chapter 6 portrays working in child welfare as 'no bed of roses' and focuses explicitly on the personal effects on workers of the strain of child welfare work. This narrative locates the workers, like their clients, as people who are abused and neglected and with little ability to resist their redefinition as mere clerks and bureaucrats. The current practice of child welfare work is portrayed as demeaning and disempowering for workers and clients alike. Chapter 7 shows how workers cope with the stress of their work. The stress of their work is played out in their bodies as they attempt to minimise risks to themselves. Chapter 8 locates this interpretation of child welfare within its historical and political context before proposing a reframing of child welfare to address the impasse in current practice. Finally, a methodological appendix sets out the process of undertaking this research, from gaining access to gathering and analysing the data.

2 Interpreting child protection

Understanding how child welfare workers view their practice necessitates a consideration of the differing ways commentators and policy makers have turned private issues of child abuse and neglect into public problems requiring a public response. The view of what child abuse is shapes and forms policy and intervention. This chapter offers a critical interpretation of opposing constructions of child abuse and neglect and locates current of child protection in historical context.

Defining child abuse

Underlying the notion of the protection of children is a model, however vaguely formulated, of what the 'effective' family (Kadushin, 1987) is. The defining of the 'effective family' and therefore what constitutes abuse and neglect have been a political process, not a technical or professional one. Different times and different cultures defined this model family in different ways. Western industrial societies, over the last two hundred years, have posited a family form based on that of the middle classes who were associated with the rise of industrial capitalism (Donzelot, 1979). Thus, the US approach to child welfare services must be understood within the culture of capitalism (Trattner, 1984; Wilensky and Lebeaux, 1965) and the privileging of middle-class family standards (Costin, 1985). Defining the best way to bring up children and the subsequent relationship between the state and the family can only be understood by analysing 'the political processes whereby (child abuse) was defined, brought to public attention, and made the subject of state intervention' (Parton, 1990, p. 8).

Gordon has identified five stages in the political construction of child maltreatment in the United States (Gordon, 1988). She places that history within the changing visibility of family violence toward women and children. The first stage (1875-1910) was the child-saving stage when family violence was defined as cruelty to children. Cruelty was defined in class and moral terms within a feminist emphasis on illegitimate male power: alcohol and depraved immigrant men were seen as the causes of child cruelty. Moral reform of the husband or institutionalisation of the children for their own protection were the solutions proposed. In the second stage (1910-1930), child welfare was defined in terms of child neglect and incorporated within professional social work. This situated maltreatment more 'scientifically' within the family's environment of poverty, unemployment, and illness. State regulation was proposed to deal with environmental stresses. During the Depression, the third stage emphasised support for nuclear families. Here, male violence was de-emphasised and maltreatment was treated by economic relief. In the fourth stage, World War II and the 1950s, the emphasis was on personality problems. This stage reinforced a patriarchal, nuclear family where the neuroses of victims, not of assailants, were treated.

The final stage, which began in the 1960s, is the second child-saving movement. In this stage, control of the definition of child maltreatment has moved away from social agencies and social workers and into the control of the medical profession. The anti-authoritarian atmosphere of the 1960s and 1970s situated the critique of family violence alongside critiques of military, political, and cultural forms of violence (Gordon, 1988). Despite this initial impetus, current themes of the second child-saving movement narrowly define child welfare as child protection (Kamerman and Kahn, 1990), divorcing child protection policies from general antipoverty policy, and targeting female-headed, poorer, minority families (Hutchison, 1992). Like the first child-saving movement a hundred years ago, the current critique of family violence has created an impetus for intervention into, and policing of, family life (Hutchison, 1992).

'Definitions of social problems cannot be divorced from theories about their etiology, correlates, and sequelae' (Hutchison, 1990, p. 64). The origin of the current, or second, child-saving movement can be traced to the work of Dr C. Henry Kempe and his colleagues at the University of Denver. In 1962 they published a paper which has shaped child protection to the present day. In that paper, based on a survey of 302 cases from hospitals, the authors suggested that the cause of child abuse was psychological, classless, and inherited. It was an illness, a 'syndrome.'

> Parents who inflict abuse on their children do not necessarily
> have psychopathic or sociopathic personalities or come from
> borderline socioeconomic groups, although most published
> cases have been in these categories. In most cases some defect
> of character is probably present; often parents may be

repeating the type of child care practised on them (Kempe, Silverman, Steele, Droegemueller and Silver, 1962/1985, p. 154).

Following the publication of this paper there was a deluge of publicity about child abuse in medical and social work literature, in newspapers, magazines, and television programs (Costin, Bell, and Downs, 1991). The construction of child abuse as a medical problem was a powerful factor in mobilising widespread concern, which further reinforced it as a medical problem. Indeed, Parton (1985) sees the rediscovery of child abuse and its marketing as representing an advance in status for a little recognised group of medical practitioners, paediatric radiologists. Many social workers and social work educators supported this medicalisation, believing in the 'special responsibility' and the 'particular skills' of doctors to detect child abuse (Costin et al., 1991, p. 323). The ready acceptance of the medical profession's individualising of child abuse as an illness is part of a long history of social work's dependence on the professional authority of doctors (Lubove, 1969). Wilensky and Lebeaux (1965), for example, have noted that medicine is the preferred model for social work as a profession and this dependence by social work serves to strengthen the link, begun in the eighteenth century, between the middle class family and its values and the values of the medical profession (Donzelot, 1979). The medicalisation of child abuse as an illness, a disease, is now the dominant paradigm in research, policy, and practice (Parton, 1985). This understanding of child abuse situates pathology in the personality of the abusing person. It ignores or plays down the social contexts in which abuse occurs.

While medical-psychological theories of child abuse still pervade and structure child welfare practice, sociological constructions of child abuse and neglect place the problem in the context of social attitudes and social structures. These views eschew the personal pathology inherent in the medical-psychological approach and offer counter constructions of why some members of society are deemed to be abused and neglected. These views can be summarised under the social deviancy, the sociocultural, and the sociosituational perspectives (Hutchison, 1990).

The social construction of child harm

The labelling or social deviancy approach is based on the assumption that behaviour cannot be classified apart from the social context in which it occurs (Hutchison, 1990). Child abuse and neglect, then, are labels that society places on parents and children who are considered to be socially deviant (Giovannoni and Becerra, 1979). Maltreatment is only considered to be maltreatment because those who have the power to label it as such, have done so. Crudely put, labelling theory implies that clients' problems are the products of social workers' biases (Gordon, 1985).

The sociology of deviance has tended to emphasise the experience of the offenders and the social construction of their deviance. In a revaluation of his 1985 publication, The *politics of child abuse*, Parton (1990) pointed to two major omissions in the use of labelling theory that undermine its effectiveness: there is little analysis of the abusive act and, consequently, there is a failure to focus on the impact of the abusive act on the child. The uncritical use of labelling theory, therefore, masks the experience of children and women who have experienced abuse.

The sociocultural approach takes into account the ways different cultural values affect parent-child relationships (Hutchison, 1990). In common with the development of the child protection movement in Western societies, our knowledge of child abuse stems almost entirely from studies of Western cultures (Korbin, 1977). Writers in the sociocultural approach emphasise the importance of an anthropological and cross-cultural perspective in the understanding of child abuse (Korbin, 1977, 1979, 1980). The purpose of this approach is to inform workers of customs from cultures other than their own and sensitise them to different ways of rearing children.

Child protection standards are set by the dominant majority. Because there are widely varying cultural and class definitions of what constitutes proper child-rearing in the United States, any definition of child maltreatment applied to all groups is going to discriminate against some cultural groups and social classes – 'the tyranny of objective criteria' as one DCFS administrator called it (Field notes, 16 July 1990). Groups likely to have their child-rearing practices devalued are those who differ most from the majority culture, the poor, immigrants, and minority families such as Native Americans (Hughes, 1987). Indeed, minorities of colour are over-represented among the poor and minority children are further over-represented among children considered abused, neglected or delinquent (Hogan and Siu, 1988). Some authors have challenged such a deficit model of social work practice (Chau, 1989; Crystal, 1989; Gould, 1988; Hirayama and Cetingok, 1988; Lum, 1982; Montiel and Wong, 1983). Generally, however, the literature on practice with minority clients is naive and superficial (McMahon and Allen-Meares, 1992). This mainly emphasises the social worker's awareness of the client as different or else seeks to help the client adapt to an oppressive environment. In much social work literature minority clients are defined acontextually without reference to the real social processes, such as racism and poverty, that shape peoples' lives.

The sociosituational approach focuses on the ways in which social structures and economic circumstances contribute to the maltreatment of children (Hutchison, 1990). For example, there is a consistent correlation between poverty and maltreatment. The vast majority of children considered to be neglected, abused or delinquent are the children of the poor (Giovannoni and Becerra, 1979; US Department of Health and Human Services, 1988; Pelton, 1981, 1989, 1991). The correlation between poverty and maltreatment has been used by DCFS workers to trace clients through Public Aid computers. One of the workers in this study told me, 'I found one (family) simply by going to the Public Aid screen on the computer and I was able to find them without knowing what the allegation (of child abuse) was' (Reid, 23 March 1992). Pelton (1981, 1989, 1991) has been a strong social work critic of the medicalising and psychologising of child abuse and neglect. He castigates 'the myth of classlessness' which sees child abuse and neglect as a disease that afflicts families indiscriminately, irrespective of their economic circumstances.

The lack of attention paid to social class in defining child abuse and neglect is often portrayed as bias in reporting, or that the poor are in greater contact with agencies that are likely to report them. Pelton rejects these arguments and makes a case for the condition of poverty itself as being a stressor that makes abuse and neglect more likely. Poverty creates a host of additional stresses on low-income families that are not experienced by the more affluent (Johnston, 1981). In Illinois in 1990, for example, 60.3% of female-headed households in Cook County with children in care had their cases opened because of a finding of neglect (Massat, 1992). Ignoring the class-based incidence of child maltreatment leads policy makers to ignore the need for changing the social context of poverty that fosters the maltreatment. Pelton (1991) further asserts that ignoring poverty as a cause of abuse and neglect has made it easier to remove children from poor parents rather than provide support services within the home.

While there is a certain validity in each of the labelling, sociocultural and sociosituational counter arguments to the disease model, the explaining away of abuse and neglect as only social constructions or biases – actions without actors – ignores the negative effects on the children who are abused or neglected. Hutchison (1990) proposes an interactionist perspective where perspectives of individual abuse in the medical-psychological tradition are integrated with sociological approaches. An interactionist perspective admits the reality of actual harm to a child and situates that reality within the socially constructed worlds of medicine, law, and public policy that make up the child welfare system.

Control/care

Child abuse and neglect, however they are socially constructed, do not come into the public sphere until official gatekeepers apply the definition to certain children deemed to need protection (Gelles, 1975). Sanction for widespread state intervention into family life is a feature of modern industrialisation. There is a complex relationship between the rise of modern Western society and the creation of defined class and age groups, including that of 'childhood' (Frost and Stein, 1989). The maltreatment of children has become defined as a social problem for which the state, rather than the family or the local community, has responsibility (Gordon, 1985). Consequently, child welfare policies and services are portrayed by some commentators as mechanisms of social control to preserve the status quo (Gil, 1985).

Child protection movements have often been categorised as examples of ruling class hegemony to control and dominate the poor (Donzelot, 1979; Piven and Cloward, 1971) by intervening in the lives of their children. The social control of family life, that is 'efforts by the middle and upper classes to manipulate and regulate the behaviour of the lower classes in order to promote the former groups' own interests, often through enhancing the capitalist system' (Trattner, 1984, p. 72), has been a central theme underlying the child welfare movement in the United States since the mid-nineteenth century. The Reverend Charles Loring Brace, for instance, through the New York Children's Aid Society which he founded in 1853, was motivated by the threat to society and property by the children of 'the dangerous classes' of New York. Brace adapted the private fostering of children into a full-scale operation, taking and sending immigrant, Catholic children out West to be trained as labourers and domestics (Trattner, 1984). Similarly, Gordon (1985) has argued in her study of the Massachusetts Society for the Prevention of Cruelty to Children, established in 1878, that its 'child protection work functioned simultaneously to control and reform *adult* behaviour and particularly to enforce or re-enforce a particular adult sexual division of labor' (p. 216. Emphasis in the original). A more current instance of control through surveillance was the harassment of Native American militants by threats of removing their children (Matthiessen, 1991). Other instances of social control are given by Lasch (1977, 1979), for example, who saw the private family 'besieged' by the intervention of health, education and welfare services. For Lasch, capitalist-industrialist society has so proletarianised parenthood that parents are now unable to act without professional help. Social control is also articulated as intervention to ensure the embourgeoisment of working class families (Donzelot, 1979).

Child welfare practice fits easily with the notion that the state is exercising control of its deviant members. According to Frost and Stein (1989), the child welfare system creates a bureaucratic supervisory regime to monitor family performance. Consider the following quotation from an interview with one of the workers in this study where, through the court and the DCFS worker, parents are compelled to abide by workers' decisions.

> If the parents do not do what I feel they need to do, and
> depending on the risk in the case, I do tell them if it comes to
> a point where you're not following through with what I'm
> asking, I will have no choice but to refer your case to the
> Juvenile Court, only because that's my responsibility as an
> agent of the department (Valdez, 14 May 1992)

Surveillance in child welfare practice is exemplified in the production of the written case file where 'social work records individualize and typify the client, the need, the situation, and the service transaction' (Kagle, 1984, p. 1). Foucault situated the development of the case within the innovations of individual surveillance, examination, discipline, and regimentation attendant on the birth of the prison, the asylum, and the poorhouse in the eighteenth century (Foucault, 1979). The production of the case is an individualising process whereby the person is 'described, judged, measured, compared with others, in (his/her) very individuality; and it is also the individual who has to be trained or corrected, classified, normalized, excluded, etc.' (Foucault, 1979, p. 191). Individual description makes the written case a means of control and domination. In the production of the person as a case, power is seen at the point where it is in immediate and direct relationship with the client. For Foucault, this is how things work at the level of on-going subjugation where subjects are constituted in subjection (Foucault, 1980).

Modern technology increases the ability of the worker to track clients and subject them to control. Listen to an excerpt from an interview with one of the workers in this study.

> There's thousands of ways to find people. If they are going to
> hold a job, you can find them; if they draw Public Aid I can get
> on the computer and pull up the Public Aid screen and run
> them down almost immediately... I kind of enjoy the hunt; to
> me it's a lot more fun sometimes than sitting in court all day
> waiting to go on in on a Progress Report, you know. Its like
> taking a photograph instead of shooting the damn thing (Reid,
> 7 May 1992).

This widespread use of computers to track and table children and families enhances a more efficient method of surveillance (Wilensky and Lebeaux, 1965) and the portrayal of the individual client as a person without gender, race, class, or family. The individualising of the client is inherent in casework generally (Kagle, 1984) and in child protection in particular (P. G. Anderson, 1989). Child welfare workers are inundated with case after case where even different children in the same family have their own file, their own number, and their own case plan. Gordon (1988) believed that the development of social casework in the early twentieth century was a rejection of nineteenth century reformism. Along with the

19

retreat from reform, child welfare casework emphasised the regulatory function of the state in the protection of children. The individualising of the person in the case became a means of domination and control (Foucault, 1979).

The social control critique of child welfare practice is useful. It has identified aspects of domination that arise in definitions of social order (Gordon, 1985). Similar criticism has been echoed by social workers critical of state surveillance and intervention in families (Parton, 1985; Wilensky and Lebeaux, 1965). But the way the social control position has been articulated by authors such as Lasch (1977, 1979), Parton (1985), Trattner (1984) and Wilensky and Lebeaux (1965), is too simplistic.

Social control explanations rely on a series of assumptions that fail to encompass the complexities of family violence (Gordon, 1985, 1988). The major assumptions of the social control position are that the family was originally autonomous, that clients are passive recipients of intervention and services, and that the family is an homogeneous unit. Gordon has persuasively argued that the notion of decreased family autonomy is a male-centred political discourse that reacts against women's and children's own rights to autonomy. In addition, her historical analysis of child protection in Massachusetts highlighted the view that clients, especially women clients, are often active initiators and negotiators in the solution to their own problems. Thus, the family is not an homogeneous unit and reification of 'the family' masks intrafamilial conflicts between male and female, parent and child.

Social control theories of child welfare, like social deviancy theories, can come to the conclusion that instances of abuse and neglect have not really happened. Thus, to give but one example, the history of prejudice and racism towards Indians should not be used to deny that Native American children are abused and neglected (Piasecki, Manson, Biernoff, Hiat, Taylor and Bechtold, 1989). A number of surveys have shown that child abuse and neglect are widespread in Native American communities (Hauswald, 1987; Lujuan, DeBruyn, May and Bird, 1989; Piasecki et al., 1989; White and Cornely, 1981; Wichlacz, Lane and Kempe, 1978) and the general environmental hazards that Indian children suffer may account for some of the cases of neglect (Hughes, 1987; Ryan, 1980).

Writing child protection

The texts that embody the representation of child protection include child welfare policies and textbooks, DCFS publications, and popular texts such as newspaper articles. These texts encode 'certainties' (Sarri and Finn, 1992) about child protection that frame its meaning within the ideology of the second child-saving movement. Central to that coding is the view of the worker protecting and saving children.

At the time of this research, there were two federal policies which underlined public child welfare practices, the Child Abuse Prevention and Treatment Act of 1974 (CAPTA) and The Adoption Assistance and Child Welfare Act of 1980 (Jimenez, 1990). These Acts were in opposition to each other. CAPTA supported professional intervention in the family in cases of suspected abuse and neglect. The Adoption Assistance and Child Welfare Act focused on protecting the family from outside interference. The two Acts encapsulated the contradictory mission of child welfare workers. Workers were mandated to protect the child by removing her/him from the family. Workers were also mandated to ensure the child was not removed unnecessarily from the family and were required to work to return children who had been removed. Jane Accardo, a child welfare worker at City Office, voiced that contradiction.

> I think our job is confusing to me because a lot of times it's to ensure these children are in a safe place. However, at the same time, it's conflicting with trying to help moms and dads get better, also. It seems to me like it's two different jobs sometimes (Accardo, 19 May 1992).

That ambivalence pervades child protective work. CAPTA received its impetus from the rediscovery of child abuse in the second child-saving movement that began in the 1960s. Congress blindly believed that mandatory reporting in itself was enough to solve the problem (Jimenez, 1990). The production of more and more cases precluded a critical stance in regard to social factors that placed children at risk of abuse and neglect. As more and more children were indicated for abuse and neglect, public criticism of social workers in child welfare practice grew. An adversarial relationship grew between clients and workers (Jimenez, 1990).

The Adoption Assistance and Child Welfare Act of 1980 was an attempt to redress the drift of children away from their biological families and to make sure that foster children had a permanent placement. This Act created standards for development and periodic review of case service plans. Central to these plans was the goal of return home for the child that each DCFS service plan started out with. The result, for the workers, of this Act has been an increase in paperwork and surveillance by review mechanisms (Jimenez, 1990). Coupled with the current increase of children entering care, the demands of paperwork mandated by the Adoption Assistance and Child Welfare Act were one of the main sources of stress for workers in this study.

Most texts on child welfare presume the reader has an understanding of child abuse and neglect. 'The child maltreatment literature contains many assumptions and theories about the consequences of abuse and neglect'

(Lancaster and Gelles, 1987, p. 10). Not surprisingly, child welfare literature written within the second child-saving movement portrayed children as victims of parental failing or mistreatment. Thus, Kadushin (1980, p. 151) wrote of the problems for children arising from 'gross parental inadequacy in role performance and from active role rejection.' Other authors also placed the problems of child abuse and neglect squarely within the medical-psychological explanation (Baily and Baily, 1983; Faller, 1981; Kempe and Kempe, 1978). Costin et al. (1991), for example, asserted that protective services

> are intended to guard children from further detrimental experiences or conditions in their immediate situations, bring under control and reduce the risks to their safety or well-being, prevent further neglect or abuse, and restore adequate parental functioning whenever possible or, if necessary, take steps to remove children from their own homes and establish them in foster situations in which they will receive more adequate care (p. 314).

These explanations locate the cause of child maltreatment in the parents and propose changing parental behaviour to protect the child. Child abuse and neglect are firmly situated in the personality of the abusing parent. The child welfare worker is an expert placed firmly in authority over the parent. The worker's responsibility is to guard the child, control and prevent abuse and neglect, and restore the parent's functioning. These constructions of the child protective role place the worker firmly in the tradition of child-saving outlined in CAPTA. An example of child-saving child protection work, from an investigator's viewpoint, is given in Richards (1992). This autobiographical work eulogises the investigative worker who battles against manipulative and lying clients, unfeeling supervisors, and unfair administrative demands to rescue and protect children.

Similarly, at the beginning of the DCFS training book for child welfare workers is a poem entitled 'Because I care' dedicated to 'Child Welfare workers everywhere.' It portrays the caring worker who protects the innocent child from defilement and injury. Removing children from their mothers for their protection is part of the job.

> I visit many homes, trying to assess
> What's happening in this family, what solution is best
> Those sweet little faces, hurt as they may be
> Don't want to leave Mom, to go away with me.
> (Gillespie, 1985)

The protection of children is a prominent feature of DCFS publicity. One brochure urges readers, 'Care enough to call. It's your chance to protect a vulnerable child from the nationwide epidemic of abuse and neglect – a social affliction that rarely stops on its own, and often grows worse with time' (Illinois Department of Children and Family Services, 1986). In this production child abuse and neglect are portrayed as an ever spreading disease that is getting worse.

In the media, the popular construction of child abuse is often formed by extreme examples of abuse or neglect (Best, 1990). Stories of rape (Levitt et al., 1992) and murder (Dugger, 1992; Levitt et al., 1992) are the stories that grab the headlines. At the same time, these horrific stories were coupled with reports of thousands of children who have 'poured into foster care in recent years' (Dugger, 1992, p. A1). Atrocity stories and exaggerated reports on the numbers of children needing protection have been the major ways in which the public has been educated about child abuse and neglect (Best, 1990). Popular culture, therefore, imitates and reinforces the ideology of child protection underscoring the second child-saving movement.

In summary, a reading of child welfare literature shows overwhelming support for the premises underlying CAPTA, that children are to be protected by investigating reports of abuse and neglect. An implicit intention of investigation is the removal of the child from the home or parental control (Jimenez, 1990). The focus on the individual protection of a child from an abusing or neglectful parent is one of the main features of child protection in the second child-saving movement. The importance of this work and the valorising, in theory, of those who do it contrasts sharply with public perceptions of child welfare work.

Dirty work

Professional intervention by child welfare workers is an ambivalent occupation in modern society. At the center of that ambivalence is the intervention of the state in the private life of families. Stimulated by a disease model of child maltreatment, the current child-saving movement focuses on physical and sexual abuse of children and on neglect. This response has seen the renewed policing of families and the divorce of child welfare policy from systemic solutions, such as antipoverty policy. The current social construction of child maltreatment now relies on a mandatory reporting system, involuntary clients, an extended network of individual case management services involving public and private agencies, and a concentration on individual caregiver deficiencies (Hutchison, 1990).

In contrast to workers' high estimation of the importance of their own work, their job occupies the lowest rank among the professions (Jacobs, 1970). Even within the social work profession the declassification of child welfare jobs and the perceived loss of control over child welfare to other professionals have lowered the esteem in which child welfare was once held (Kadushin, 1987). In addition, public agencies are now becoming service managers rather than service providers. Child welfare workers negotiate with private agencies for services for their clients rather than engage in direct service provision (Born, 1983). While this can be rationalised as a more holistic and ecological approach to practice (Esposito and Fine, 1985), in reality it can be an often thankless task of juggling a multitude of providers (Stein, 1987). It is not surprising, then, that workers feel they lack agency, peer, and public support (Esposito and Fine, 1985). Child welfare work is an illustration of what is called 'dirty work' or work which has to be done but is distasteful to do (Blyth and Milner, 1990).

The nature of child welfare work does not endear clients to their workers. Gordon (1988) mentioned how clients hated child protection workers, even when they were helped, because the clients rarely got what they wanted but what the worker interpreted as their need. This ambivalence goes to the root of public perceptions of child welfare. At one time, child welfare workers were lauded as the safekeepers of America's children. Their status as respected experts has diminished over the last 30 years (Esposito and Fine, 1985). The double bind that must balance the interests of the child and the privacy and autonomy of the family lays them open to being attacked and pilloried if they make a false step either way (Frost and Stein, 1989). Now, newspaper accounts of social workers who are too lenient towards clients or, conversely, too mean and hard reveal a public antipathy to the dirty work child welfare workers do (Edwards, 1987). The public abuse of welfare workers, for which they have little recourse, is a recurring theme in the Chicago press (Cuadros, 1991; Greene, 1991).

This chapter has reviewed the literature that sets out the (current, limited) social construction of child welfare and child protection. It has briefly traced the origins and ideological underpinnings of child welfare work, showing the importance of protecting children from harm and the essential ambiguity inherent in child protection. The next four chapters convey an interpretive understanding of child welfare work at city Office. Chapter 3 introduces the eight workers and portrays their understanding of their work. In Chapter 4, the workers speak about the counterproductive effects of their practice on many of the children they are protecting as they try to come to grips with the contradictions in their work. Chapter 5 shows how the demands of child welfare work are bureaucratising the professional relationships between workers and clients. Chapter 6 focuses explicitly on the personal effects on workers of the strain of child welfare work.

3 Protecting children

Workers' own stories about their reasons for going into child welfare practice and their friends' reaction to what they do, placed them as child savers leading exotic and dangerous lives. In owning 'this romantic ideology' (Denzin, 1992, p. 44), an ideology inscribed in DCFS texts and child welfare literature, the workers were able to frame their work-purpose as the protection of children-victims. This chapter introduces the eight child welfare workers in City Office through their own biographies. Guided by Denzin (1989a; 1989b), this chapter gives an interpretative understanding of their work from their own point of view. Significant events, or epiphanies, within each worker's life situate and structure the understandings of child welfare work. Since it was through the biographies of Native American clients that I came to the workers' understandings of what they do, I situate their Indian clients within the biographies of the workers. Clients' biographies, filtered through the bureaucratic rendering of their lives in filenotes and visits, are examples that portray the workers' understanding of child welfare practice.

The eight workers in this study were spread over three of the seven teams in City Office. Typically, public child welfare workers at the direct service level are predominantly young white women without professional social work education (Corby, 1987; Hegar and Hunzeker, 1988; Kadushin, 1987). However, these eight, four men and four women, ranged in age from 28 to 56. Two had Bachelor's degrees in social work and two others were studying part time for their Master's degrees in social work.

The missionary

Arlinda Delval, a vibrant woman in her early 50s, had one Native American family case, a Menominee father and his five children. She had 55 cases altogether and had had the Indian case for six months. It was transferred from another worker in her team who had gone on maternity leave. In this case, after a number of indications for neglect brought about by the mother's addiction to 'Tolly,' a paint thinner, the father requested DCFS' involvement when he had an accident at work and was unable to care for his children. Arlinda was working to return the children to him, 'little by little.' She admired what the father was doing: 'he seems very concerned for his family, very appropriate with his children. He had to learn how to self-control, but for a 29 years old father with five children, he's doing tremendously well' (Delval, 15 June 1992).

Arlinda's work was shaped by her life as a refugee and as a mother. She was born and married in Cuba and had been working for DCFS for ten years. On and around her desk were pictures of her daughter in her First Communion dress and mementoes of her family and of Cuba. She told of the trauma of leaving her native country: 'I live in Cuba until the Communists took over and then I thrown from Cuba to United States, thrown with nothing, just with whatever I knew in my brain.'

Arlinda and her husband have a son who was born in the United States and a daughter they adopted. She has a Bachelor's degree in sociology with a minor in psychology. Her child welfare work was defined by the refugee experience of children snatched from their families. In her case, the 'snatching' of her three miscarriages, which she attributed to the events in Cuba, was part of her experience of being a refugee.

> The first people who came to suffer in Cuba were the children. They had to be separated from their parents and sent to the United States because when the Communists took over in Cuba the parents sent the children to the United States alone to be received here by the Refugee Center and placed in foster homes. You know, the aim at that time, was that all the children would be sent to Moscow to be trained as soldiers. And that's why all the Cubans sent their children to the United States. So maybe that was the beginning of me, now, because I suffered with all those children coming to the United States by themselves. It was very traumatic. And maybe one of the reasons why I lose three pregnancies because I was anxious to be a mother but I was afraid that my child would be sent to Moscow. And I lose three pregnancies. They were all boys. I was full three months pregnant so we knew they were boys. Finally, I had my boy here; he had to go nowhere.

In Cuba she was a school teacher and a catechist for the Catholic Church but she resigned when Castro came to power; she refused 'to teach the children lies about doctrine against God and against my own feeling.' When she came to the United States, instead of continuing as a teacher – 'I saw the children, they were kind of wild' – she decided to work with families, first with [the Illinois Department of] Public Aid and then with DCFS. She saw her work in explicitly religious terms, literally as a mission. She believed her caring for clients would bring them to God.

I like lots to help people. I think it's maybe because of my faith. I'm Catholic and I was always trying to gain people to the Church and the best way to gain people is to work with them, to satisfy their needs, to cover their needs, to help them in their crisis. You care for the person in crisis, you care for the person when they need it, you show them that you're there for them because that is what is going to bring them to God.

She carried her sense of mission into her private life where she worked with a group of women to provide meals and shelter for the homeless during the winter and she took Communion once a month to elderly people in a nursing home. When asked to define what purpose she saw for her child welfare work, she defined it, first, in terms of protecting children by taking them from their families.

I feel the children are the victims of the grown-up people. Protect children, that's my definition, protect children, from any risk, from any risk. If it means that they have to be removed from their parents, I say some parents have to learn how to be a parent.

Not surprisingly, because of her background, she was also a person who valued keeping families together.

You see, in almost all our cases, the children suffer separation. (I) try to help the parents to get together with their children. The life to be stable and just stuck together; to be with their children, to be there for their children.'

When she succeeded in reuniting families 'I see the heaven that day. When I don't succeed I feel sad.' Her work is 'like a mission to make children happy and bring families together again.' 'I do be positive and optimistic when I work with my clients. I see the possibility that they can turn around and do better.' Arlinda's work touched the dilemma inherent in child welfare work, saving children from abusive families while trying to work with those same families to return the children in safety.

In keeping with the idea of mission and vocation in Arlinda's definition of work, she believed a worker must be personally committed to establishing relationships with clients and must be prepared to work hard. She offered this advice:

Get to know those people. Don't look at the people, your client, as I'm here and you're there. Feel like you are there to help them. This is a job that a person has to be committed to. Social services is not like an accounting job, not like a film critic; in social services you have to work for people, people with a lot of misery and a lot of problems.

Her experience had been that other people, such as her friends and acquaintances, appreciated what she did, even if they didn't want to be the ones to do it. 'The people see that fathers abuse their own daughters and see the need that there has to be a system to protect that child from that abuse and send the father to jail' (Delval, 15 June 1992).

Delval's articulation of child welfare practice mingled a number of themes. There is strong emphasis on the protection of children. She has little doubt about the importance and necessity of her work. Having experienced family separation in her own life, she worked to return children to their families and 'sees heaven' when she can do that. In our conversations, Arlinda conveyed to me her optimism and her sense of religious mission. Her life appears motivated by a sense of service for those less fortunate than she. Personal relationships are important to her. Her advice to workers is to become closer to their clients – 'don't look at the people, your client, as I'm here and you're there.' She wants parents to create the same closeness with their own children, 'to be there for their children.'

Helping take care of children

Erica Kane had a caseload of 62 including six Native American cases in two families. In one family with three children in care, 'the mother was drinking and she would leave the children home alone while the father was working.' These children, aged four, eight, and nine, were in three different foster homes. The parents, the mother is Chippewa while the father is white, had been generally cooperative in working with Erica. She had had this case for over a year. The other two Indian cases were a ten year old Winnebago boy in a residential placement and his mother. This boy's mother had been very uncooperative, even hostile, with Erica and the previous worker. Erica had had these cases six months.

Erica Kane was in her mid 20s, the middle child of three children. Her mother was in insurance and her father was an attorney. Erica graduated with a Bachelor's degree in sociology and then worked for a year in an insurance company. She had been with DCFS for four years. Erica was influenced to work in child welfare by her older sister who worked at a daycare center and had looked after a small boy for over three years. Erica valued her work for DCFS as an opportunity to work with children although initially, she said, she 'sort of fell into' working with DCFS.

> I know I wanted to do something in the personal services, human services field and DCFS was the one I thought I would be most interested in. I had applied for a job with the state as a social services career trainee. I knew that I liked children but I didn't really have anything particular that lead me to this, it just sort of happened and kind of fell into my lap and I took it (Kane, 15 June 1992).

Like Arlinda Delval, she believed she was there to protect children, 'by providing services to help their children grow up in a little more safe manner than they ever have been' and then to reunite families. Her liking for children, especially small children, was evident in her visits to them. When I accompanied her to visit clients I was struck by her focus on and attention to the children. Her concern for children comes through in what she wanted to see in families so that children can be returned home: 'I think just helping them see that here are other ways that they could take care of their children without having DCFS in their lives . . . So it's something that definitely needs to be done and I think the idea of doing that appeals to me.'

For Erica, a preeminent consideration was to get parents to change their child-rearing patterns. She believed that the type of person to do child welfare work was one who was interested in helping people, one who wanted to make a difference in the world, yet one who was firm and in control. She spoke of nurturing her adult clients, as well as making sure they did what needed to be done.

> Nurturing to a certain extent the children but also some of the parents sometimes, but you need to be firm about things, you know, about what needs to be done and you need to stay with the plan and not let the clients talk you around, talk you out of things.

This had been hard for her and working for DCFS had changed her. She had grown more forceful in making sure clients 'get back on track.'

> I think I've gotten more aggressive, certainly in my driving (laughs) but also just in dealing with people. People start, they're talking to me and they're wandering around in different points and you know, I take a little more effort and get them back on track, and things like that. I think I'm also a little more (pause) short-tempered or something.

Erica saw the necessity for DCFS workers 'to have some control in the family's life.' Unfortunately, she said, her clients didn't always see the necessity for what she was doing. Parents didn't cooperate and she felt that going to court and doing paperwork got in the way of doing her job. The day-to-day reality of her work in some way tarnished the 'ideal' of helping children.

> Its hard, you know, in real life, you don't always have people that are cooperative and pleasant to work with, and you have all these other things getting in the way, like court all the time, and you know, all these time constraints, and all the other paperwork. So that kind of takes away from the ideal job situation of trying to do this kind of work.

Like Arlinda Delval, Erica related the awe that acquaintances had for the work she did. Like some other workers when I asked them what others thought of their work, Erica relaxed and smiled, enjoying the celebrity status of child welfare work. She told me,

> They get very solemn like 'Oh wow, that must be really hard' (laughs). So I say, 'Yes.' (They say) 'Oh that must be really depressing' and they get all serious (laughs). So I just kind of nod my head and agree.

Being known for having an interesting, even a dangerous job, with its high ideals of saving and protecting children was important to Erica and to other workers in this study.

Erica's love of children and the necessity to protect them was coupled with a firm belief that parents need to be made aware of what they can and cannot do. She admitted that being a child welfare worker had made her more aggressive but she was reassured in her stance by the importance of her work: the perennial child welfare issues of protecting children and reforming parents blended again in Erica's work.

The lifer

Janine Cooper shared a corner of a room with Erica Kane. Their desks merged together. On the wall above them was a large notice board covered in photos of children from their caseloads, Janine's young daughter and her pets, and, in one corner, a headline from a supermarket tabloid that told the story of a baby who supposedly survived six weeks in a pumpkin. Janine had 61 cases and among the photos are two or three of her Native American case, a four year old Chippewa boy born with Foetal Alcohol Syndrome. 'This child had probably the worst case that [the hospital] had ever seen. He weighed only two pounds at birth and he's pretty severely retarded. He has a lot of breathing problems . . . He's four years old; he only weighs 17 pounds (Cooper, 27 March 1992).'

Janine described herself as 'a Midwestern type,' who was born in Chicago and had no wish to move. Her father was a tool-and-die maker and her mother a secretary. She was one of four children; her two brothers were in business and her older sister, a social worker, ran a daycare center. 'I had always been interested in what my sister was doing and she had been doing all sorts of things back then, working for the National Organisation of Women and going on marches and things. So I was kind of leaning that way, I just needed a push (Cooper, 12 May 1992).' That push was a trip into the city she took with her high school sociology class in her senior year.

> I grew up in the all-white suburbs and we took a trip into the city. I'd never been on the 'el' (elevated) train before. That was interesting – subway, graffiti, gangs – things I was never exposed to. We took the 'el' all over the southside and the westside and it just kind of opened my eyes a little bit; it really made me think. It was the different types of people. Different races and backgrounds. We got off and we walked around. We also took a trip, with my Spanish class, into a Hispanic neighbourhood. When you take the 'el,' you're going through people's backyards and you're looking basically at pretty impoverished areas. It really was an eye-opener. You just read about things like that when you're living in Wheeling or Buffalo Grove.

She had been thinking of becoming a teacher but after those two trips she decided on social work. After graduating with a Bachelor's degree in social work she worked in daycare, which 'required no experience and paid nothing.' 'But I always liked being with kids and taking care of them, and I loved taking care of babies. I did that for a year, took care of eight; it was wild. And then I started getting a little bit more experience and I decided to take the test for DCFS. I wanted something that paid a little bit more.'

Janine was in her early 30s and was married. She had one daughter and was expecting another child. Most noticeable, in speaking with her, was the love and attachment she had for some of her cases. Poignantly, she realised that some children are hurt by the impermanence of the child welfare process itself.

> I just had to transfer, God, like a week ago, these kids I've had for five years. My supervisor really wanted me to send it up to another unit and I've been begging him not to. I went to say goodbye the other day and it's really hard because I was involved in taking them from their mother, I was involved in sending them home to their mother, I was involved in taking them away again. There's always been this one person at DCFS who knew them and now I'm gone.

This type of concern for children, where she makes a longterm commitment to oversee their cases, typified Janine's work. In the new influx of cases, she had already identified some children who had been shuffled around in the child welfare system and she was already planning to make sure they had at least one site of permanence in their lives, herself. 'There's a couple (of new cases) I think I am going to hang onto simply because they have been thrown around a lot and I think I can take them through the next couple of years till they turn 21.'

Janine spent a lot of her work getting parents to understand that there are certain things they need to do, either to get their children back or to keep their children at home. She conveyed the impression that she spent time working with parents, building relationships with children. Thus, she valued being a follow-up worker because it meant she can help parents. 'I'm not the one who usually takes custody of the kids. I'm not always the bad person; I'm kind of the person that's going to help them get the kids back.' She believed a child welfare worker has to be a good motivator, 'you can be something of a friend to them.'

Originally, Janine did not see herself as working a long time in DCFS, but she had come to describe herself as a 'lifer,' in DCFS for life. She joked that when she's 50 she would still be going, 'but in a walker because I'll be so tired.' She said she had no energy at the end of the day. Yet, despite the draining nature of her work, she found it fulfilling. Child welfare work had a sense of purpose and accomplishment which she doubted she'd find any place else.

> You don't have that much success but there's the sense of purpose and, I don't know, these lives are just so fragile and it's so sad. But you can kind of take somebody's life that's real messed up and even if it's a baby, you know, one with cocaine in its system, you can somehow set something right. There's a sense of fulfilment in that that I don't think I'd get if I was working getting the ledgers straight (laughs) (Cooper, 1 July 1992).

She, too, noticed that others think she has a dangerous and exciting job.

> People kind of look at what you do and they think, 'Wow, that's really great.' I go to these boring functions with my husband and they're all mad scientists working with numbers and things like that 'Wow, you go to Riverside Meadows? Wow, that's dangerous' (laughs). It's kind of funny how other people react to it.

But she was not as amused by other people's reactions as she once was. 'I don't get excited about it anymore. The families start to sound the same, the problems all start to sound the same, and the successes are so few.'

Janine valued building relationships with the children on her caseload. She couldn't do it with all of them so she searched out those whom she thought needed her the most. These were usually the children who were moved frequently from foster home to foster home or children, like her Indian case, who were badly wounded. She treasured time to build relationships with her clients and she fought with her supervisor to create that time.

Just commonsense

On the second floor of City Office were three members of another team with Native American children and families on their caseloads. This team was unusual at City Office in that almost half the workers in the team were male.

David Casey's desk lamp had a large 'Notre Dame' football sticker on the shade but there were few personal touches to his office. David was first introduced to me by his supervisor as the office expert on Native American clients. His expert status derived from the number and complexity of Indian cases he had had over the eight years he worked at City Office. At the time of the research, four of his 57 cases were children from the same Menominee family. Three of the children were cleared for adoption by relatives. The fourth child, a newborn, remained with her mother. The first two children were indicated for neglect. The latter two were indicated for abuse in that they were both born with traces of cocaine in their bloodstream.

David Casey, the son of an electrician and a telephone operator, was born in Chicago and had spent most of his 40 years there. He was married and did not have children. After graduating with a Bachelor's degree in history, he worked as a construction worker before beginning work with DCFS. He did not recall any urgent need to work for DCFS; his choice was more personal, he needed a job. 'There were bad economic times in '83 and '84 and at the time I didn't have a job. I was hoping to get a State job, I took the test, and found out that there were openings in the child welfare area, so that's how it really started (Casey, 12 May 1992).'

He didn't pinpoint any particular motivation for child welfare work. 'You know, the thought appealed to me and the job was available so it pretty much went like that.' He worked for a year in a DCFS boys' shelter. 'I had to have a year there to be qualified to get a caseworker job.' Working in the shelter kept him closely involved with children. Follow-up work was different. '(Here) you're in charge of the whole thing instead of just working with the kids in their day-to-day living arrangements.'

For David, child welfare work meant dealing every day with children who have been mistreated. 'I don't know if there's much worse in the world than an innocent child not receiving what they need. (Also), there's always a possibility of them getting hurt and just on a personal level, that's hard to take.' Yet, stressful as it is, the work was 'pretty satisfying' when you knew you've helped someone 'and that happens, it really does.' However, satisfaction was not an everyday occurrence and depended, as it did with

Janine Cooper, on working with clients over a long period of time to bring it about: 'Like you've been working with a teenager for four or five years and they tell you what you were saying is right, or if you have a family and you can see a dramatic change in the way the parents relate to their children. You would see that occasionally, so a lot of it is the ability to stick with people for a long time.'

When I asked David Casey who was the ideal person to do child welfare work, he replied that the person had 'to have some real basic humanity and empathy for other people' as well as 'be kind of tough and hard-edged' because the thin-skinned can't do the job. His supervisor put it more bluntly, good child welfare workers are born, not made: 'I've had workers like, maybe suburbanites, it takes them an incredibly longer time to work the streets and to know and to sense things. I think when you grow up in the city it makes it a lot easier; you kind of have this street sense' (Interview, 6 December 1991). For Casey, innate street sense was too simplistic an answer. The most important thing for the worker was to have some 'good, old commonsense.'

> You are going to have to learn how to deal with a lot of different personalities, people coming at you from different ways. (That means) we have to deal with our administration. We have to deal with other agencies, the court system, the clients and that's divided into the parents, the children, the foster parents and everybody has a different point of view on almost every issue. So we have to juggle all these and try to make sense and get everybody headed in the same direction. I want to go back to commonsense again; you can't expect too much from people and you have to realise that the system itself has all these inherent obstacles but you have to find a way to work within all those obstacles and barriers (Casey, 22 November 1991).

Casey's description of child welfare work emphasised that it is often a process of negotiation. Whereas Erica Kane could state that she expected people to do what they are told, Casey placed practice within layers of negotiations. He articulated practice as a series of juggling feats to 'get everybody headed in the same direction.' He delineated his understanding of child welfare practice as an extremely complex and tortuous obstacle course.

Interestingly, Casey proposed that 'commonsense' rather than expert knowledge is the means to negotiate the obstacles that constitute child welfare practice. Commonsense, the understanding of the problems and pressures clients have, is situated in the worker's own biography and personal experience rather than in academic learning. 'I think the more experience you have, the more different things you have been exposed to, are going to help you in this job. It might not be something you learned in social work school.' This commonsensical understanding of child welfare sees practice as the carrying out of technical tasks.

Nobody has a Brady Bunch family

Jane Accardo has three children from a Kiowa family among the 73 cases on her caseload. These are the first Indian cases she has had in her two years with DCFS. The oldest child in this family was indicated as neglected. The other two were born with a positive indication of cocaine in their systems. The baby is also HIV positive. The oldest and the youngest were being cared for by their maternal grandmother. The middle child was in a specialised foster home because of health problems.

Jane, a woman in her late 20s, was born in the northwest suburbs of Chicago, the sixth of eight children. She had a Bachelor's degree in social work and was studying for her Master's degree in social work. Her father died when she was ten and her mother ('she was pretty much a housewife') struggled to raise three girls and five boys. Jane's biography was shaped by the hardship of her own childhood. As she said, 'Nobody has a Brady Bunch family, I guess.' Jane was married and she had no children of her own.

Her childhood played a major part in her decision to be a social worker. When she first went to college she tried nutrition and fashion merchandising but was drawn to social work. 'My father died when I was really young and my mom struggled – she also had a problem with alcohol – and basically we raised ourselves.' From her own experience of need came her desire to help others, especially children. 'I always wanted to help people, probably from that. I think a lot of it is upbringing and wanting to just give back or help make it a little easier for somebody else' (Accardo, 19 May 1992).

After graduation she worked in a group home for adolescents in the suburbs 'and it was a pretty horrible experience.' She 'wasted' nine months before getting a position working with the elderly. Although she did that for some years, it still wasn't what she wanted to do. She then joined DCFS because 'I wanted to work with kids.' Despite the hardship of her own upbringing, she spoke with amazement of the lives her clients lead. Their need, and her own background, were the spurs that drive her on.

> I really had no idea it was like this when I was growing up in the suburbs. My picture of the city people was a lot different. I just can't believe there are so many people, so many people that are in this situation here in Chicago. People on the news are our clients, you know. People being shot and killed and

murdering people are people that we know. You always listen to the news thinking this is far off somewhere else and it's not.

Her own upbringing was divorced from that of the clients she worked with, 'the city people.' While there was no identification with the clients, her work has mollified her response to her own upbringing. 'I mean the background that I had is still like a million times better than the kids' that I work with. I guess I appreciate my life and maybe it wasn't as tough as I thought it was, seeing what these kids have to go through.'

Her friends, she said, share the same ignorance, and the same wonder, that she originally had about working in the city. When I asked her how she explained her work to other people, she told me she got a similar reaction to Erica's and Janine's. Her friends, too, want from her a voyeuristic tour of 'the city people.' 'Everybody seems to want stories, major stories. I mean they always look at me like, 'Oh my God, what you do is just outrageous.' I try to think of some interesting stories but they always look really shocked.' While Jane said her friends picture her going into client's houses and grabbing screaming children, she tried to dispel that false idea of her work. She told them of the types of people who are her clients and how negative drugs are: drugs are 'a lot of reasons why these kids are where they're at. That and just being young, generations and generations of being poor and not having the opportunity to do anything.'

At the same time, Jane enjoyed the busy-ness of the work, the variety, the people – 'the week goes by really quick. It's never boring.' Not for her a quieter, less hurried life. 'I can't imagine sitting in an office and typing all the time, eight hours a day.' She needed to work at something that is important to her. 'The few times that you really can feel good is when you are able to help somebody. When I get up in the morning there's a purpose, whereas a lot of my friends can't say that.' Working in DCFS gave her that sense of purpose. She also valued the salary, the insurance benefits, and the possibility of going to graduate school.

Jane presented herself as task-oriented, a woman who did not suffer fools gladly. She could never be accused of wasting time. When I asked Jane what three things you need to know to work for DCFS her answer encapsulated a description of herself. 'I'd say, number one, organisation. You need to be an organised person or you're just wasting time. Two, I think you really need to have some compassion and really want to work with people. Three, it's helpful to know the paperwork, rules and regulations, because it really makes your job easier' (Accardo, 30 June 1992). And, she added, 'to be a lawyer, a doctor, have 15 degrees and a really good memory helps.' In contrast to David Casey who emphasised the experiential knowledge needed for child welfare work, Jane valued expert knowledge alongside experience. The theme of protecting children came though Jane's description of her work: it's important for her to have this sense of purpose in what she does.

Fighting for the rights of kids

Bob Heenan shared an office on the second floor with Taina Aponte, the worker who grew up in the neighbourhood. Bob was a thickset man in his mid-40s given to wearing garish ties when he dressed up for court appearances. Above his desk was a map of the world framed with postcards and photos of places he had been. On his caseload of 65, he had two Indian cases, a Yankton Sioux boy and a Winnebago girl, both teenagers. Their stepfather dropped them off at a police station saying he could no longer look after them. The boy was fostered by an Indian family in Kansas. The girl lived with her sister in Uptown, a cosmopolitan neighbourhood on the northside of Chicago where many Indians lived. These two cases were abruptly transferred to Bob when another worker resigned. He has had Native American cases before.

Bob Heenan grew up in a working class Irish-Catholic neighbourhood in Chicago. An only child, his parents were divorced when he was two years old and he lived with his mother, 'a fairly unreasonable woman.' 'I can remember when I was a kid saying that I wanted to fight for the rights of kids. Kids get no rights. I used to think it was very oppressive the way she treated me and I wanted to do something about it' (Heenan, 2 June 1992).

Bob's mother worked as a secretary and his father was a police officer. He graduated from college with a Bachelor's degree in psychology ('a useless degree') and went to work for the Illinois Department of Public Aid. He was in the Protective Service Unit that visited the aged, the blind, and those reported as abused and neglected. He chaffed at the petty rules in that department – 'you couldn't use your mind at all in Public Aid. You had to only go under these real simple formulas that went against reality.' He transferred to DCFS in 1979. 'A lot of people went over at that time and they all said it was real hard but you'd feel better about yourself doing it.'

> Part of the reason I think I did it is I was sort of caught up in the hippy movement and social change in the 60s and 70s and I never had any ambition to make money or to be real competitive in a capitalistic way, so I thought if I was going to do anything that would be important, it would be for social justice or a just cause, and I saw this as one.

In 1987, DCFS received unflattering media coverage and some workers were fired. Bob became frustrated with his work and quit his job. He spent a year travelling abroad. He did not want to come back to DCFS after that but the harsh reality of the need for a well-paying job forced him. 'I just had to grin and bear it.'

Bob had noticed a change in DCFS since he began working there, a change he did not see was for the better.

> When I first came here there was more of a personal kind of counselling that went into what you did with people. Now it is more informational. You just meet them and say that you need to go to a counsellor. You can tell them a few things to do and more or less how to play the game rather than really seriously discuss why you are there and why you are in this situation and that it is not a game. You just don't get time to do that now (Heenan, 2 July 1992).

Despite his frustrations with the job, he liked the seriousness, the importance of it. 'I like the fact that it is serious, that it is an important thing to do. It's frustrating but since somebody has to do it I just think it is a worthwhile challenge.' The importance lay in the making of decisions that effect the lives of children, 'whether to take them away and whether to return them.' Yet, experience, reflection, and a continuing series of newspaper reports that portrayed the negative effects of foster care and of separation from families on children had convinced Heenan that less intrusive intervention was necessary.

> I think they have to admit that they can't do what they originally thought they could do in the late 70s, that they could have a Hotline that would protect all children from their parents. I mean you have to try to some extent but we've gone overboard. I think we shouldn't take kids unless they're in danger of serious injury or death, not just (lacking) a good life. Nowadays, we'll take them for any kind of reason and, you know, once we've done that it's so hard to undo (Heenan, 2 June 1992).

Bob had noticed a change in the way the public understood his work. When I asked him how he explained his job to other people, he told me, 'I'll just tell then I'm a social worker because I don't want to tell them I work for DCFS.' "When I first started I was fairly proud of it and I used to tell them I work for child abuse, I work for the State. They'd all want to ask questions. They would say, 'Oh, that must be a tough job, but I'm really grateful that you do that. I couldn't do it but it's a real good thing that you're doing it.'" This comment parallels the experiences of Erica Kane, Janine Cooper, and Jane Accardo. Now, their acquaintances no longer have the same awe of their work.

> I haven't heard that for three or four years. When I used to say (what I did), they'd act like you're a missionary or something.

Now, they've read so many articles in the papers, they look at
you like a stiff. They think you've screwed up somebody's life.

The paramount theme in Bob Heenan's biography was the protection of
children; he was still 'fighting for the rights of kids.' But he was saddened
by the change in child welfare practice over the previous decade. Bob's
nostalgia for a return to a more 'personal,' more 'serious' child welfare
practice fuelled his conviction about the deterioration of child welfare
practice in Cook County. He rejected the promise of universal protection for
children exemplified in technological solutions of the previous decade, such
as the Child Abuse Hotline. He regretted the passing of a time when
workers were able to establish a professional rather than a bureaucratic
relationship with their clients.

The hunter

Arthur Reid was on the third floor of City Office. Like the workers on the
second floor, his office was a converted bedroom. Arthur Reid was in the
same team as David Casey, Jane Accardo, and Bob Heenan. Arthur's
caseload of 63 included seven Native American cases. Two Menominee
children, a boy aged ten and a girl aged eight, had parents who were 'severe
alcoholics. We got these children when they'd been left for a minimum of 24
hours alone in an apartment without utilities, no heat. The children were
covered with lice, there was no food in the house and they hadn't eaten for
several days.' They now lived with their tribal 'aunt.' Another case was a
ten year old Menominee girl who had been sexually molested by her
grandmother's boyfriend. She had told her aunt about it and she too was
now living with her aunt. Finally, two boys, one a Winnebago and one a
Chippewa, were indicated as neglected by their mothers. They were living
with their respective grandmothers.

Arthur Reid was in his mid-50s. He was born in Colorado where his
father had been a highway engineer and his mother a schoolteacher.
Because of his father's work, the family once moved 21 times in two years.
'We lived like nomads across Kansas and Oklahoma.' During World War II,
they settled in Kansas where his father bought a hardware store and then
had a stroke almost immediately. 'Things kind of fell apart for a while.' He
worked fulltime through high school. 'I began to identify with the
underclass. I recognise what a lot of these people are going through.'

When he was fifteen years old, the Korean War broke out. He was already
in the National Guard, having lied about his age. 'I would probably have
been killed with the rest of them but somebody in my family jumped on a
congressman and they had me out. I got to California with the troops and
didn't go any further.' Arthur joined the Navy and served in Taiwan, Korea,

and Vietnam. After the Navy, he worked in the defence industry, then as a child labour investigator in Wyoming and at a vocational training facility in Montana for the rural disadvantaged. Much of his work in Montana was with Native Americans. He had a Bachelor's degree in business management and a graduate degree in public administration. He worked in Chicago as a training officer for an insurance company before joining DCFS.

Arthur's involvement with child abuse began when he was working in Montana. His wife edited a small newspaper and reported on a number of cases of severe child abuse. But it was while his wife was in hospital after a miscarriage that he became interested in protecting children.

> I guess this had a big part of it. My wife had lost a baby and was in the hospital. Down the hall was a woman who lived only about five or six houses from us who refused to accept this child she had just had. Well, the nurses kept saying we wish to hell we could give her to you because you'd take care of her, we know that... A report came back later from North Dakota that this little baby had been taken into the hospital and dumped on a desk; she was only about 4 months old and she'd been raped. The mother had run in and dumped her there... so when our son was born we spoiled the hell out of him... I like kids, I set up my tool box in front of my house and repair the bicycles and the wagons and the scooters and all of that. My dad used to do the same thing (Reid, May 7 1992).

Arthur Reid was meticulous about what he did. He prided himself on reviewing cases and closing them. Like the other workers he valued the independence of his job, but he also enjoyed the testing of wills and skills with attorneys and clients. A descendent of a famous frontiersman, Arthur framed his relationship with clients in hunting terms. Once hunted and found, he trained clients to do what he wanted.

> You've got to have a lot of patience. You've got to have some tenacity, for instance just in finding these people. Running these people down can be really hard and you've just got to stay with it. Then, when you find them, a lot of them are not about to work with, meet with you. I'll go by at 7.30 in the morning a few times and pull them out of bed and after I've done that three or four times then I can come by at nine in the morning and they would be there after all. That's what it takes (Reid, 23 March 1992).

Arthur had worked in DCFS for five years, including one year at City Office. For him, 'You've got to like kids or you couldn't do this. It's more than a job. I don't think anybody can do it if it's just a job. It makes DCFS palatable in a sense.' 'People who don't know anything about my job, if they find out what I'm doing, they say, 'Someone's got to do it, but thank

God I don't have to do it, thank God you will.' Its like they're talking to a garbage man or someone' (Reid, 7 May 1992).

While he subscribed to the importance and necessity of his work, and the stress of it – 'the cops tell me they wouldn't do what we do' – Arthur did not like to publicise what he did. Like Bob Heenan, he had experienced the change of public attitude regarding child protection and DCFS and the downgrading of what he did. He particularly resented his work being used as a legal bargaining chip.

> When DCFS started up we were considered saviours; now they hate our guts. I don't tell people where I work. I made the mistake of telling a few people, neighbours, and some of these old Italians want to tell me of allegations of abuse by their sons-in-law. Some lawyers tell women that if they want the money and they don't want anything to do with the son-of-a-bitch to make a complaint to the Hotline. It's wrong but that's what they do (Field notes, 10 June 1992).

Other acquaintances wanted titillation. "And then you get the psychos who say, 'Tell me about the sexual abuse. Do women do it, too' and they start this stuff" (Reid, 7 May 1992). Arthur preferred to keep his place of work a secret, saying only, as do many of his co-workers, that he worked for the state.

Arthur had had a lot of experience working with people. Talking with clients is his specialty. On visits, he joked with the children and negotiated and haggled with their mothers to get them to do what the court required. He had worked with members of a number of different Indian tribes and was sensitive to the cultural differences and customs between one tribe and another. Alongside Arthur's genuine commitment to protecting children was the joy of the chase. He liked to take on hard cases and then explore all the avenues he could to bring the case to a successful conclusion. He was tenacious in following a lead using computers, written records, and a long memory to track clients.

Making a difference

Also on the third floor was Juan Valdez, a member of a third team. Juan had one Native American case, a fifteen year old Chippewa girl who had been sexually abused by her stepfather. During the five years since this had occurred, the girl had lived in non-Indian foster homes until, more recently, she had been 'bouncing around different relatives in Chicago,' mainly her mother's sisters.

Juan was in his mid-20s and had been working for DCFS for one and a half years. He had 60 cases on his mainly Hispanic caseload. Juan was born in Colombia and came to the United States when he was three years old. He was the middle child of three children and got his interest in helping people from his father, a pastor who worked with Hispanic immigrants in Chicago: 'He did a lot of work in kind of integrating people into society and hooking them up with services, jobs, housing, things like that. So I was able to see the gratification that he got from that and I felt that I wanted to do something like that . . . I think the one thing that I derive from my growing up is dedication' (Valdez, 14 May 1992).

Yet, when he was growing up, it was Juan's mother whom he could count on. 'My mother is steadfast, kind of the rock.' She was an accountant, 'very logical, steadfast, organised. I think back and I remember that growing up it was my mother that I knew I could count on. My father was always out.' Juan said he takes after his father, but has a little of both parents. Like Arlinda Delval, Juan's own immigrant experience has reinforced the idea that keeping families together was very important. 'I think that comes a lot from my culture, from my own family. When we got here we were all we had.'

Juan had a Bachelor's degree in Leisure Studies. After graduation he worked in a park district in Missouri and, although he was working with children as he wanted to do, he felt it was not enough. He decided to move back to Chicago in order to study for a graduate social work degree. While he was in Missouri, there were two incidents that made him determined to become a child welfare worker.

> The family that impacted me the most was one where I could see the parents were trying to the best of their abilities, you know, but I think they had more children than they could handle. The entire family was about six kids. It was just seeing these children come to the center on a daily basis, sometimes their clothes weren't the cleanest and sometimes they'd always be a little hungry and I always had something in the refrigerator for them. It just hurt me personally to see that on a weekly basis. Plus, while I was down there, I had done some reading on my own into child development when I was in college and I started to see what was going on in society. I felt I wanted to serve as, I guess, an impetus for change.

Like five of the other workers in this study, Juan was married but had no children of his own. His child clients filled that place in his life. 'Every time friends ask me if I have any children, I tell them, not of my own, but I feel sometimes I have about twenty.' Family was important to Juan. It was so important that he was prepared to risk censure with DCFS administration and to lobby the attorneys at the Juvenile Court for families on his case load.

> If a mother is making progress, I'll talk to the Public Defender
> and I'll tell them what the mother is doing so that the Public

42

Defender can be an advocate as well as me. If a child needs certain services that I am having a very difficult time getting through the department's structure, then I will talk to that child's Guardian ad Litem (a court appointed lawyer that represents the child's interests) in court and tell them, 'Hey, I'm doing the best I can. Now I need you to put some pressure on.' If I have to fight the system and possibly cut my own legs off, I will do it to get what I need. I know that if it comes down to losing my job, let's just say that I know my skills are marketable.

Juan saw himself as dedicated, committed. 'I always try to do extra stuff' such as keeping in touch with children he has had to remove from their parents and place in foster care. 'I do make (cases) personal. I do put in extra hours . . . I think what I like the most is meeting different people. Especially the kids. I feel I'm making a difference for these kids.'

Juan placed a lot of emphasis on reasoning with people, talking with them to convince them. This, his clients have told him, was in contrast to other workers who ordered clients to do what the court required. Backing his reasonableness, however, was the knowledge in both worker and client that it was not a voluntary relationship. Behind both was the power of the court to decide on the removal or return of a woman's children. 'I do tell them if it comes to a point where you're not following through with what I'm asking, I will have no choice but to refer your case to the Juvenile Court.'

Like Arlinda Delval, his Cuban colleague, Juan placed a high value on keeping families together. The Anglo workers said as much but I was impressed with the feeling with which the two Hispanic workers told me of their belief. For both of them protecting children seemed to be tied closely to protecting families. Juan, however, wanted to do more than just protect children, he wanted to make a difference for them.

Qualifications and training

The rhetoric of child welfare, enshrined in textbooks and policies, is that child welfare practice is an important part of social work. 'The profession of social work is the single profession that is most clearly identified with the field of child welfare' (Pecora, Briar, and Zlotnick, 1989, p. iv). While this may be so historically, those who do child welfare work are not usually social workers. What sort of qualifications did staff need to be a public child welfare worker in Illinois? Officially, the requirement was a Master's degree in social work, or a Bachelor's degree in social work supplemented by one year's professional experience, or a Bachelor's degree in any field, but 'preferably related to social work,' supplemented with two year's professional social welfare experience (Vacancy notice, 11 June 1992). In fact, as Bob Heenan said, the degree 'could be in art, it could be in dance' (Heenan, 2 June 1992).

Are the City Office workers typical of child welfare workers generally? A 1987 US study of public child welfare personnel found that 28% of workers had Bachelors or Masters degrees in Social Work and 70% were non-Social Work graduates (Lieberman, Hornby and Russell, 1988). Very few states require any professional qualification for child welfare workers (Dubray, 1991). The eight workers in this study had a variety of college degrees. Arthur Reid had a Master's degree in Public Administration. Arlinda Delval had a teaching qualification which was not recognised in the United States. She also had a Bachelor's degree in Sociology, as did Erica Kane. Juan Valdez had a Bachelor's degree in Leisure Studies, David Casey had a Bachelor's degree in History, and Bob Heenan had a Psychology degree. Only two workers, Jane Accardo and Janine Cooper, had Bachelor of Social Work degrees.

The reluctance of graduate social workers (MSWs) to work with involuntary clients and in public child welfare is well-documented (Pecora et al., 1989). Two workers had opinions on why graduate social workers were not common in DCFS. Bob Heenan thought that those with an MSW degree, a group he saw as ambitious for their own careers, did not stay with DCFS because 'it doesn't mean anything here. You won't be promoted any faster with an MSW than without one.' For David Casey, the lack of MSWs in DCFS was not because of personal ambition but because MSWs did not want to do public child welfare work. 'They would rather be in less well paid private agencies than in DCFS. The reason, he thinks, is that DCFS is the point of last resort; they have to take the kids that no one else wants' (Field notes, 26 March 1991). Both explanations portrayed graduate social workers as elitist.

Since new workers will often join the department without knowledge and experience of child welfare work, DCFS provided a period of 'core training' to prepare new workers for the field. David Casey noted that core training is helpful, 'but a lot of the things you learn in training you don't understand how they apply until you really get out into the field and start experiencing that' (Casey, 22 November 1991). Further training was mandated, at least 20 hours every two years. Workers had mixed reactions to these sessions, full of praise for some, scornful of others. Most enjoyed the opportunity to meet colleagues and socialise with them. For half the workers in this study, these workshops were their only source of professional child welfare materials. Arthur Reid and Arlinda Delval told me they did read professional child welfare literature outside workshop sessions. So, too, did Jane Accardo and Juan Valdez who were pursuing graduate degrees in Social Work. Workers, therefore, typically learnt child welfare practice from doing the job.

The following interview with a young child welfare worker, the least experienced in the study, highlighted the process whereby a worker was initiated into the job of being a child welfare worker. Juan Valdez admitted he was still learning; 'I come up with situations that I've never had to deal with, so every day is a learning experience for me.' In his learning, he identified three elements that produce the 'good' worker, talking with other workers, reading departmental policy, and going with his heart.

> A lot of the learning I did was just talking with the other
> workers on my team. I spent the first few months just talking
> to other workers, getting some guidance from them. I did a lot
> of reading in terms of policy, articles that my supervisor would
> give to us. And then, basically, when I started getting assigned
> cases, I went with my heart, you know. I did what I thought
> was best with this case and usually, it wound up being what
> was the correct thing' (Valdez, 14 May 1992).

When I asked Juan how he knew what was the correct thing to do, he replied, 'I guess I base it on my background and what I saw when I was growing up, and on my parents.' In his answer, practice wisdom, social work values, and cultural, religious, and class values blended to structure practice. Again, workers' understandings of practice came from their own biographies and their identification with the ideology of child-saving. Valdez's positive understanding of his upbringing for practice can be contrasted with the negative childhood experiences of Jane Accardo and Bob Heenan. Either way, their self-stories served to reinforce the ideology of protecting children from what Jane Accardo and Bob Heenan knew, or saving children so they could experience what Juan Valdez knew. Their childhood experiences gave coherence and meaning to these workers' lives and to their child welfare practice.

This chapter has introduced the eight workers in this study, their place of work, and their own understandings of what they do and why they do it. The workers framed their practice within the ideology of child-saving that is typical of the second child saving movement. Native American clients played minor parts in the huge caseloads workers had. Two significant themes emerge in this chapter from the stories of the workers. The themes are child protection and the importance of relationships with clients. That child protection is a theme is to be expected from child welfare workers whether the idea comes from their own biography or whether they have accepted it as a now central component of their work. The importance for some workers of relationships with their clients also emerges. As Janine Cooper and Bob Heenan said, however, relationships with clients are at odds with the current working practice of the Department.

In the next chapter I will propose a view of practice that is in opposition to what child welfare workers and child welfare texts have said they understand by child protection. Drawing from the workers' descriptions and understanding of what they do, I will argue that the division between what is proposed for children and what actually happens to children produces negative consequences for them similar to abuse and neglect.

4 Punishing kids

In this chapter I move on from workers' stories about their own understanding of child welfare work to describe their understanding of the people they work with, the clients. Stories of triumph over the odds by individual clients sustained and guided the child welfare workers. These stories justified their work and reinforced workers' belief in child protection and their own sense of purpose. Stories of individual triumph fitted neatly into the ideology of child-saving. In contrast, workers related how the reality of child welfare practice could be harmful and damaging to the clients, both the children who are protected and their families. Many of the problems children had in foster care were a result of being taken into care. The disjuncture between what was proposed for children and what actually happened to them produced negative consequences for children that were similar to abuse and neglect. The chapter will focus on three topics to highlight the negative effects of foster care: the effect on the child of placement itself, the instability of placements for many children, and the frequent transferring of cases between workers.

Individual triumphs

The eight workers told me they don't see much success in what they do. Yet each had a number of stories of clients' triumph over adversity and circumstances. For the workers, these stories served to counterbalance, with glimmers of hope, the often discouraging nature of the work they do. The following example by Arlinda Delval was typical of the stories the workers told me. Central to each of these stories was a long-standing personal partnership between the worker and the client. All the stories I was told were of female clients.

I have one child who was abandoned when she was six months old and her therapist requested that I continue to be her worker. Right now, she's 20 years old, she's still with me. The only worker she knows is me and I refer her to different agencies and she doesn't want to deal with them, she only wants to deal with me. Maybe because she was so attached to me or maybe because she doesn't like people in her life. She's independent, she's kind of hostile, she's still hostile to the idea that her parents abandoned her. She will be now at college, so she's working hard to be someone in the future. I laugh, two weeks ago I talk to her and I ask her, 'What are you going to be studying there?' and she said, 'social worker.' I don't know, maybe she got a good role model or maybe, I don't know, she's very hostile child. So I don't know if she's going to be a social worker. Maybe, it will help her; maybe she will help other people, same like her (Delval, 15 June 1992).

Stories of individual triumph serve to reinforce and make real the child-saving and protective purposes of child welfare work used to frame workers' achievements. The stories also countered the popular understandings of what child welfare workers do. They negate the popular construction of the workers as child-snatchers and family-destroyers. The stories linked the problematic nature of child welfare practice to the child-saving ideology that surrounds the discourse of child protection. In that way, individual triumph stories served to further legitimate, on a personal basis, the work that child welfare workers do. Stories of individual triumph created personal measures of success for individual workers.

Arlinda Delval's story of the personal triumph of her young client goes further. She linked the story of individual triumph to her client's choice of career, social work. In that way the girl's story begins to parallel the biographies of the workers in this study. It is as though this client has served a novitiate to prepare her for the same type of practice that Delval values. The girl's life experience as a client builds, for Arlinda, a circularity that makes sense of the client's life. Arlinda proposes her own interpretation of an epiphany in the client's experience of abandonment that will frame the girl's life and work. This epiphany, coupled with the idea of herself as a role model, creates sense for Arlinda from what the client has experienced and reinforces the importance of her work.

The major frame used to view and explain the workers in this study was the current meaning of child-saving given to the public issue of child protection. Each worker, social worker or not, experienced or not, female or male, believed in the necessity for her/his work of protecting children even if some disagreed on the details of the appropriate way of carrying it out.

The next section outlines 'a typical day' before considering the workers' negative understandings of their jobs.

A working day

David Casey insisted to me early in my research, that it is working with children already in care that takes up a follow-up worker's time. I had been asking him the process whereby children come into care when I mentioned foster care. His response was intense: 'He leans forward and speaks emphatically. 'This is what we should be talking about,' he says, 'not about the process of kids coming into care.' Most of his time is spent with placement problems and with fosterparents   (Field notes, 26 March 1991).

DCFS child welfare services were referred out to other agencies, either to those with a contract with DCFS for certain types of service such as counselling and therapy, or to community agencies such as county mental health agencies. David Casey told me that 'The job of the DCFS child welfare specialist is to monitor the provision of those services to the child and the family. A child welfare specialist can't do direct practice unless he/she is a licensed social worker.' Follow-up work meant ensuring that clients get the services the court has ordered them to receive. The client is expected to accept these directions, whether they come from the court or from the worker. Bob Heenan outlined his work with clients.

> Basically, probably the most important thing is to get them with good counsellors, good services, whatever types they need and just give them a good understanding of what they need to do and what they don't need to argue about. Other than counselling and services we don't do a lot directly for the clients, except talk to them in so-called counselling (Heenan, 2 June 1992).

A job vacancy advertisement for a Child Welfare Specialist II in a follow-up team noted that a worker 'performs a variety of casework management functions related to the welfare of children' and that 'duties are performed in an independent manner.' This independence appealed to Jane Accardo. Her 'casework management functions' were divided into three sections of child welfare work: office work, visiting clients, and going to court.

> First of all there is no typical day, which I kind of like about this job. A lot of the times I like to get in the office at least once during the day if possible to see what is going on, pick up my messages, handle any emergencies that come in, go over my mail, and start scheduling visits and working through cases. There is always something to do. I will be on the phone a lot during the day and it will be ringing. And filling out forms in

between doing three things at a time usually. This would be a typical office day (Accardo, 19 May 1992).

Despite Jane's protestations about there being no typical day's work, there are certain functions that workers have to perform each week. The 'typical' working day in the office, then, can be a frenetic blend of writing and phoning. Time is short and not to be wasted. Workers continue reading files or writing while carrying on conversations. The same organisational strategy was transferred to visiting clients. 'When I'm in the field I like to do the visits all on certain days. If I know I'm going out to a certain area, I will try and visit whoever I have out there' (Accardo, 19 May 1992).

Workers were required to visit most clients once a month. As client numbers grew, the burden of the monthly visit increased. Workers did not visit for long. Of the times I accompanied workers to visit their clients the longest visit was 57 minutes and the shortest, one minute. Most client visits I observed lasted between ten and twenty minutes. Quick visits to clients contrasted with the time spent waiting in Juvenile Court. 'Court day, a lot of the time, is a waste of time. You will go in and you will have to wait. You have to be there and wait for the judge. So many hours are wasted in the court room' (Accardo, 19 May 1992).

Workers resented having to come early to court and then have to sit around and wait. Often, two or three members of the same team were sitting and waiting for their cases to be called. Workers routinely returned to City Office complaining about the wasted time spent at Juvenile Court. Pithouse (1987, p. 45) remarked on the workers he studied that they 'seek to control the pace of their activities.' My interpretation was different: 'I don't get this sense (of control) at City Office. Their activities are dictated by court hearings and crises. They often work at their desks over lunch. They work after hours: Arlinda said she was talking to a weeping girl on the phone at 6.00 p.m. last night. Taina Aponte said surprise visits (to check on clients) are mandated (by the court) and this often means outside work hours, including weekends' (Field notes, 14 May 1992). My impression of workers at City Office was that their work activities structured the pace of their lives, not vice-versa.

'The system punishes kids'

There are increasing numbers of children entering the child welfare system (J. Anderson, 1990; Hardin, 1990). As many as 500,000 children, nationally, were predicted to be in care by 1995 (Kantrowitz et al., 1991). Younger (J. Anderson, 1990) and more troubled children (Kamerman and Kahn, 1990; Stein, 1987) are placing enormous strains on the child welfare system. While child welfare workers strived to help children who needed protection, they resented the steady flow of cases across their desks.

> We've gone so far, we're overboard. I think basically we shouldn't take kids unless they're in danger of serious injury or death, not just (lacking) a good life. And nowadays, we'll take them for any kind of reason and once we've done that, it's hard to undo. We take them for slap marks on their butt or something. I mean, that isn't that serious. It's abuse and can be looked at as that, but it shouldn't mean remove them (Heenan, 2 June 1992).

National trends about the overwhelming numbers of children coming into foster care are repeated in Illinois (Stehno, 1990), especially in Chicago. At a further interview, Heenan elaborated his views on interventions that typically result in children being taken from their parents.

> It is not a good solution in general to take kids away from their parents. I believe it is done way too much and it should be only done if there is great danger; for instance, if there is a fractured skull, or if there was someone hanging a kid from the window. It would have to be some indication that there was going to be some danger to a child.

In continuing his critique of child protection as it is currently practiced, Bob Heenan placed state child welfare intervention as social control of the deviant: 'Nowadays, kids get taken away because their parents kept a sloppy house and scream at people who tell them not to. Until they aggravate them enough to take their kids away or they don't show up for some appointments that an authority figure sets for them' (Heenan, 2 July 1992).

Contradicting the workers' understanding of the protective nature of their work was their dissatisfaction and agitation with what happened to the children who had been placed. Bob Heenan continued his critique.

> While the idea of rescuing kids from trouble is nice, what happens, once they become a ward of the state, is indelible, especially if it happens too young. Sometimes, if they get adopted they can get out of the system, they can escape it. But if they stay in it, they stay in foster home and continue getting services from the state and move around from place to place and display behaviour problems. They are going to come out a troubled, troubled adult. At least as troubled as if they'd stayed in a crummy house (Heenan, 2 July 1992).

Typical of workers' stories about what happened to children once they entered fostercare was the following account from Arlinda Delval. The story illuminates the counterproductive themes inherent in child welfare practice. In the account, the parents are both portrayed as abusers, although the use of alcohol does not seem to have become relevant to the definition of abuse until after the father sexually abused one of his daughters. They way Delval tells the story, the placement of the children precipitated their negative behaviour. (In her telling of the story, she does not mention that the sexual abuse itself may have been a contributing factor.)

> Back, like three years ago, I have a case that the mother was American Indian and the father was Mexican and they have three daughters. The father sexually abused the oldest child and the mother was alcohol abuser, so was the father. So we had to take in custody the three children. The children were placed with private agencies. Then the behaviour started to deteriorate. The father has a sister and she wants the children to be placed with her. We placed the children with that paternal aunt and they did well for about three months. Then they started acting out. The paternal aunt requested to remove from her house.

Workers have many stories like this, stories that seem to indicate that children are worse off after removal from their home than they were before. Such stories rarely have a happy ending. 'I heard the children are still in the system. I left that unit and I saw the worker working with the children not long ago and he told me that two of the three daughters are pregnant and still wards of the state. Mother was working towards getting the children returned but she used too much alcohol' (Delval, 15 June 1992).

Arlinda finished this story by blaming the overall system of child welfare: 'We are failing our children. Not as a worker but as a system in not providing foster parents committed to our children.' For her, blame lay not with the worker, nor even with the foster parents, but with an amorphous 'system.' In this story, she defined the source of failure as the lack of better recruiting and screening techniques for foster parents.

Erica Kane told a similar story. Three young (4, 8 and 9 years) Chippewa children were left alone while their mother was drinking. The children were indicated as lacking supervision. Their father was at work. The two boys – the youngest child is a girl – were originally placed together in a non-Indian home but the younger boy was removed from the foster home because 'he was just having a lot of problems and the foster mother didn't want to deal with him.' Problems included bedwetting and defecating in his pants.

> The father tells me that some of it had been before, not the bedwetting but the defecating in his pants. The father says that he was doing much better in school (before) and wasn't having the same kind of problems with other kids as he's having now. The older boy is in counselling right now because when he first came to the foster home he was a little withdrawn and he was also having some problems with other kids. (The girl) doesn't

seem to be having any problems at the foster home. She's adjusted very well. Although she does miss her family, she seems to have just adjusted well to the foster home (Kane, 20 March 1992).

In this account, the negative results of placement – bedwetting, defecating, trouble at school, withdrawn behaviour – are more explicit than in the family mentioned earlier. A connection had been made, by the worker, Erica Kane, and the children's father, between their placement and their trauma. The placement was blamed for causing the trauma. Yet, a further comment is necessary. The girl's adjustment to her foster home, without apparent trauma, which was portrayed by Erica as positive, is in contrast to the negative portrayal of the boys' behaviour: the foster mother of the middle child 'didn't want to deal with him.' A positive telling of a foster placement fits neatly with the ideal of child protection, that children are saved and protected. There had been no failure in the system, in Arlinda Delval's terms, because committed foster parents had been provided.

Trauma associated with placement is understandable in small children, even in older children. The traumatic effect on children of their removal from their families was called by James (1979) the quiet violence of care. Jane Accardo: 'a lot of cases you will notice that the behaviour problems will usually obviously relate to the fact that they are separated from their parents and they are not dealing with that real well' (Accardo, 20 March 1992). Workers, like Juan Valdez, were not comfortable with this. Not only was it a further traumatising of the child but, in some fashion, the child-victim was punished. His description of placement in the following account recalled one element of the definition of an institution, 'you are being told what to do all the time.'

I've seen so many children that are just devastated from being removed (from home). These children, especially if they're young, and even adolescents, just can't cope with the fact that they no longer have a mother. In their eyes, they don't have a mom, you know, they're a foster child. And my personal feeling is I don't feel comfortable putting any child through that . . . Once you come into placement, you're being told what to do all the time. In a way, it's not motherly advice, it's just downward authority, because these children know that this isn't my mother. In my opinion, it's worth the extra effort to maintain the family because I see what happens to the kids once they're put in the system (Valdez, 14 May 1992).

James (1979) listened to foster children and noted their suffering when separated from their families: 'I have been able to glimpse what it feels like to have no birthright, no claim on anyone or anything as your own as of right . . . not to know where you'll be living in a year's time or where you were living three years ago' (James, 1979, p. 62). Further burdens were placed on some children by the medicalisation of those considered difficult children. Understandably, foster mothers were not keen to have children placed with them who cause problems, children like the boy who was bedwetting and defecating. He was assessed further: 'What we are doing is getting a psychiatric evaluation done on (him) to determine if he needs hospitalisation because of his problem, because we've had a request in for foster care for a long time and no one wants to take this boy' (Kane, 20 March 1992).

Demands were also placed on the worker. She was obligated, as the excerpt infers, to obtain a more permanent foster placement for her cases. Sometimes, the practice seemed to be, when in doubt what to do, evaluate. Speaking of the four year old Chippewa girl who adjusted so well to her placement, Erica Kane said, 'So the counselling agency wanted to do an assessment on her just to determine whether or not she needed treatment.'

For Native Americans, of course, a central issue in having the Indian Child Welfare Act passed into law was the same drifting away from their families and tribes of Indian children placed in care. However, of the 27 Indian children in DCFS' care at City Office, 18 were with Indian relatives or in Indian foster homes and nine were in non-Indian homes. This ratio of Indian to non-Indian foster homes for Indian children was nearly twice as high as the national ratio for Indian children in foster care (Plantz et al., 1988). As well, most workers knew the tribe the Indian children on their caseloads belonged to. It is worth noting in this context, however, that four of the 27 Indian children at City Office were misidentified as 'white' in a DCFS computer printout given to me in August, 1992 although the case workers of these four children were well aware of the children's Indian heritage.

One conspicuous exception to the workers' knowledge of their Indian clients was the case of an eleven year old boy in a residential setting who had been asking DCFS and private agency workers for a year and a half to find out which tribe he belonged to. At the staffing (six monthly review meeting) I attended, the staffing report noted, 'Tony also shows much interest in his Native American background and we will continue to try to locate his tribe in order to attain these benefits' (Field notes, 18 May 1992). He was experiencing what one Indian commentator called a form of cultural deprivation injurious to his development as an Indian child (DuBray, 1991). Neither the staff nor the DCFS worker appeared to be making an effort to keep Tony in contact with his tribe. The low priority given to his quest for knowledge of his personal and cultural identity was not because the knowledge was hard to find: two weeks after attending Tony's staffing, I was able to ask one of the Native American workers at an Indian child welfare agency about Tony's tribal affiliation. She knew of

Tony, knew his tribe, knew his mother, and was able to describe his large extended family. (This information was passed on to the relevant worker).

Fragmented services

David Casey said to me one day that it takes 50 people (court, child welfare workers) to look after one client. He was exaggerating but the diverse services clients received, the turnover of staff serving them, and the serial pattern of foster care for many children, meant that each client interacted with a number of ever-changing, variously agenda-ed service providers. Jane Accardo, as an example, listed the workers that a Kiowa mother had to deal with. There was Accardo for the three children, the mother's probation officer, at least two drug counsellors, a visiting nurse, and someone from each of two Indian child welfare centres (Accardo, 20 March 1992). Other families had similar experiences of fragmented service provision. 'I have a different case where there is one child in the adoption unit, one child who isn't and there's two DCFS workers, plus many private agency workers' (Kane, 20 March 1992). This fragmentation of services was also a problem for other players in the child welfare process: 'I think that's what the judges at court get a little irritated with because there's a gap of service there when you transfer, there's things that aren't done and there's things that are done differently, you know, when you change to a new worker that worker doesn't have the visits the way the other worker used to do. And the parents don't like that, the judges don't like that. It becomes a big problem' (Cooper, 1 July 1992).

Within the same agency, there was often a high turnover of workers, whether that agency be state or private. David Casey thought the cause of the high turnover of caseworkers in private agencies was due to the need to earn a better living. '(Private agencies) pay a lot less, and people are always looking for better opportunities. You don't see many people in the private agencies we deal with that stay there for long periods of time; (they move on) even more so than us' (Casey, 22 November 1991). Clients were very aware of this movement of workers. One 14 year old Chippewa girl told Juan Valdez on his first meeting with her that he was the fifth worker she'd had in four years (Field notes, 17 June 1992). This girl's comment recalls the experience of impermanence of Richard Cardinal, a 17 year old Chipewyan Indian from Alberta, Canada, who hanged himself in 1984. Cardinal had been taken from his family at the age of three and had had 16 different sets of foster parents over the next 14 years. His handwritten diary titled 'I was a victim of child neglect' was found after his suicide (Cardinal, 1991). A short video, 'Richard Cardinal: Cry from a diary of a Metis child,' recalls his life and death.

Not only were there many, ever-changing workers from different agencies working on the same case, children were moved from foster home to foster home. Characteristically, Bob Heenan made that point bluntly.

> Once we get these kids, we take them out of marginally bad situations from their parents, we put them in with strangers and we move them three or four times. They already have learning problems and they don't get along with other kids at school, and they get more disturbed and more disturbed. We have teenagers, they have no connection to a family, they have no upbringing, they have no one that is consistently instilling values, and they're just loose cannons, and they really can be in trouble. You know, we've created monsters (Heenan, 2 June 1992).

Thus, for Heenan, the disruption and change in much foster care exacerbated rather than helped an already damaging situation. Change, instability, and uncertainty arising from placement further traumatised and demoralised already abused and neglected children. Arlinda Delval saw this climate of uncertainty and instability as a further betrayal of the children who already felt abandoned by their parents. 'I don't like the idea that our children go from one worker to another worker and then they feel betrayed by their parents, they feel betrayed by their worker' (Delval, 15 June 1992).

Case goals that require the movement of foster children through a pre-determined set of organisational checkpoints make explicit a rationalistic understanding of child welfare work and add to the instability. Within this framework, the service, not the service provider, is important: it does not matter who provides the service as long as the service is provided. Administratively, services were constructed as the providing of individual actions without personal context. This (bureaucratic rather than professional) frame of reference created a moral disjuncture for some workers.

> These aren't everyday kids, you know, they already have all these different things, people that they've had to say goodbye to and people that they've left, so I think that when you can provide some of the continuity you should. You know, if we are going to say you shouldn't haphazardly move children from home to home, (then) we shouldn't haphazardly transfer them from worker to worker. And, it's hard on the parents, too, you know. I don't think as much about them as I do about the kids sometimes, but they don't like to tell their whole lifestory over and over again, either (Cooper, 1 July 1992).

The need to move children through the administrative system was driven by the continual influx of new cases into DCFS. Without a focus on moving eligible cases on to other sections of the department like adoptions, workers were swamped with an ever-expanding caseload. 'When we have a chance to transfer cases (our supervisor) makes us do it. It doesn't matter if you're attached (to the child), it doesn't matter what your reasons are, they go. He's like, don't come crying to me when we're two workers down and your caseload doubles' (Cooper, 1 July 1992).

Despite admitting the practical and legal reasons for moving cases along, Janine Cooper believed that a more permanent relationship with one worker was advantageous to a child. 'I've noticed in children that I've had for a long time a sense of stability in them. To have one stable person . . . does make a difference' (Cooper, 12 May 1992). Not only did she believe it was good for the child, Janine also believed it made achieving the case goals easier. Continually changing cases from worker to worker frustrated the attainment of case goals.

> I just think that when you can (hang on to a case) it just helps provide a sense of continuity for the family; it's easier to return children home; it's easier to put them in the more permanent placements like adoption. A lot of the (previous) work gets stopped (before) it gets started again by a new worker. We're finding that now with cases that were just transferred to us for a few months. I haven't done very much with them because there's the knowledge that you're probably going to transfer them back to someone else, anyway (Cooper, 1 July 1992).

It appears that a consequence of current child welfare practice was that some children received their primary sense of stability and coherence from their caseworkers. Thus, for many children going into foster care, the unavoidable trauma of being taken from their families was compounded by the provision of services that were fractured and disjointed. This disjointed provision of services flowed from the administrative construction of child welfare work as a technical skill needing any worker to provide the required service. This idea/policy was at odds with workers' notion that unstable children also required stability and consistency in their home life as well as in their contacts with professional organisations.

There is a contrast between the romantic ideology of child-saving in the previous chapter with the reality of child welfare practice. The disjuncture between what is proposed for children and what actually happens to them produces negative consequences for children that are similar to abuse and neglect. Many of the problems children have in foster care are a result of being taken into care. Three topics, the effect on the child of placement itself, the instability of placements for many children, and the transfer of cases between workers highlight the negative effects of foster care and emphasise the counterproductive effect current child welfare practice has on abused and neglected children.

5 Boilerplating

This chapter considers what workers understand as appropriate behaviour for their adult clients, the perpetrators of the neglect or abuse that the children have suffered. What workers consider appropriate responses from parents are fashioned within the meanings workers give to the terms parent and family. Central to this chapter is a critique of the behaviourism which drives and undergirds child welfare practice. Behaviourist, bureaucratic practice treats clients as a passive, homogenous, generic group. Child welfare work becomes mere documentation, displayed in an homogenous boilerplating of clients' individualities and workers' expertise. Clients, however, reject this view of themselves and resist their silencing.

Making clients

It is sometimes confusing who the clients of DCFS are. Jane Accardo told of her own confusion when she first started as a child welfare worker: 'They're all our clients (parents and children). Although I didn't think that was going to be the case when I came here. I thought I was going to be working with kids (Accardo, 30 June 1992).' Children become clients of DCFS through being indicated for abuse or neglect. Adults are also clients of the department and workers construct theories about being an adult client.

For adults, there are a number of elements involved in being made a client. First, a parent, usually the mother, must acknowledge a need for help. Second, she must display what is considered behaviour appropriate for a parent and not display behaviour which is judged to be inappropriate for a parent. This behaviour, since it may not have been familiar to her, must be learned and she has to go to parenting class to learn it. Finally, she must learn and display appropriate behaviour according to the notion that what she is doing is voluntary behaviour.

Jane Accardo intimated that her interactions with clients within the frame of her protective mission as a child welfare worker formed her feelings toward them. Clients who resisted 'what is best for them' or who sought material assistance (which DCFS doesn't provide) rather than psychological or therapeutic help were seen as behaving negatively and inappropriately. And there were times when she felt negatively toward clients. 'When they're hostile and when they are really angry and mad at DCFS as a whole, and they want us to do something we can't do for them. A lot of times what they really want us to do is give them money and we just can't do that.'

Underlying this worker's negative attitude to her clients was their refusal to do what she wanted them to do. 'You set them up with everything really ideally and they just say they are not going to do it. That makes me mad, it takes me a while to cool off after that. I guess they don't realise how they are set up sometimes and (that) it is for the best for them. They can't see that; it's so frustrating' (Accardo, 30 June 1992)

One consequence of the workers' negative reaction to clients' resistance was the development of a worker-client relationship that was the antithesis of the therapeutic relationship. The element of a trusting verbal relationship, essential to professional therapeutic interaction, was lacking.

> I've learned to not trust any of my clients, which is sad. (Laughs) I mean there are a lot of things I just don't believe, because they all lie to you. Even in the closest relationship you have with a client and how much you've helped them, really even for no reason, they'll lie to you (Accardo, 30 June 1992).

Arthur Reid did not have the same high expectations. He concentrated on what clients did, not on what they said. He saw clients as needing different standards of behaviour to survive.

> When you're out there talking with these people they're lying to you. You should expect it and you shouldn't get angry. I've seen people get angry because they say I trusted him or her, they lied to me. You've just got to expect it; you've got to know that the only thing you can trust, you can believe, is what they do, not what they say. If they're going to their rehabilitation program and they're going to Parenting Skills classes and the kids are getting fed and the house is looking better and the children are going to school, then things are looking up. You're looking at what's happening and not what they say. That's not just cynicism (on my part), that is a protective way, that's how they survive; they've been lying to everybody all their life, they have to (Reid, 1 July 1992).

The emphasis on what clients do, and the ability of workers to make clients do what they have to do, is the foundation of the rehabilitative side of child welfare practice. Having clients do certain prescribed behaviours has continued to be the measure of what workers, and courts, construct as appropriate parenting. It decides whether workers are doing their job and whether mothers will get their children back or not. Behaviour that the worker approves of as being appropriate parenting behaviour results in benefits for the mothers of children in care, benefits that result in having their children returned to them.

> When they really show it, that they want help and they are showing an effort, they're putting in an effort towards themselves, I mean I will bend over backwards for a client like that. When a person really wants to make their life better, that really motivates me (Accardo, 30 June 1992).

Clients need to show their dependence and their effort to workers. Jenkins and Norman (1975) in a study of 128 mothers of children in care found that the mothers thought there were five types of behaviours that workers valued in clients. These were to be undisguised (honest and frank), to be controlled (in regard to feelings), to display concern for the child to prove to the worker that they were concerned, to be formal (reserved, distant, polite), and to be acquiescent (accepting the workers' decisions, cooperative). Clients who did act appropriately were rewarded with extra services and, ultimately, with the retaining or the return of their children.

Behavioural procedures are widely used in child welfare work and in social work. Like Arthur Reid's stressing what client's do, the behavioural approach places emphasis on what can be observed. As a theory of human behaviour it is anti-introspective and against the use of constructs such as meaning, motive, intention, or self (Denzin, 1987). This makes it problematic for the interpretation of child abuse because it ignores the position of meaning or motive in the social construction of abuse and neglect. Despite these criticisms, behavioural procedures play a large part in the social construction of the abusing/rehabilitating parent. As is apparent, these child welfare workers distrusted behavioural means of assessing the change in parents even as they continued to rely on them.

How did workers judge whether involuntary clients had really changed the attitudes or behaviours that led to their children being indicated as abused or neglected? The ideal client was an acquiescent person who did what she was told if she wanted her children back: 'If she wants to be a mother she's got to act like one. This is what it's all about' (Reid, 7 May 1992). Workers were not necessarily interested in how the parents understood their redefinition as abusive: '(Nowadays, the workers) just give them a good understanding of what they need to do and what they don't need to argue about. You know, a lot of parents just want to argue over and over again whether they're good (parents) or not, which is really not the question' (Heenan, 2 June 1992).

However workers phrased it, getting clients to do what 'they need to do,' defined by the service plan, was a central part of child welfare work. On the one hand, motivating clients could be, in the gentle words of Erica Kane, 'Just helping them see that there are other ways that they could take care of their children' (Kane, 15 June 1992). Or, on the other hand, motivation could come from the threat of court action, 'I do tell them if it comes to a point where you're not following through with what I'm asking, I will have no choice but to refer your case to Juvenile Court' (Valdez, 14 May 1992).

The emphasis on behavioural indicators of parental fitness was reinforced and compounded by the Juvenile Court's regular ordering of routine treatments for all cases. Arlinda Delval related her experience of perfunctory court-ordered services. "If the kid is under three (years), put him in a 0 to 3 program', not even knowing anything about the case. 'She's 16, she has a psychological problem', whether they need a psychological or not" (Accardo, 20 March 1992). Arthur Reid reported the same thing, 'The judges always want counselling, they always want Parenting Skills classes and we tell the (clients) they have to go and we make them go' (Reid, 7 May 1992).

Cooperating with the service plan was the only way for a mother to have her children returned to her.

> There's almost a generic plan for everybody. I mean, if you take away a kid, you refer the (parents) right away to a counselling agency, it doesn't matter who, and you see how regularly they go. If they go regularly after a matter of time, their therapist will usually recommend that the kids be returned. Now, I don't know what change happens in any of those situations, but usually it's more a matter of a person playing that game, cooperating with their therapist, making the therapist like them at least a little bit and trust them a little bit, and eventually they will get their kid back (Heenan, 2 June 1992)

According to this account, the interpretation of any client's transgression and of any client's rehabilitation is told and retold in terms of one typology of abusing and neglectful parents and one typology of rehabilitative services. One plan fits all and all clients have the same plan. Instead of the case report individuating each case (Foucault, 1979) the generic service plan homogenises all clients into one.

The following series of recommendations was typical. It was from the case file of a five year old Chippewa boy who was indicated for neglect. He had been left crying in a car while his mother was in a bar.

Mother to understand and correct conditions which led to neglect, through counselling. Mother to submit to a substance abuse evaluation and engage in whatever treatment is recommended. Mother to visit her son regularly and display appropriate parenting skills (Field notes, 15 June 1992).

This extract displays a number of terms that encode behaviour required of a client. The mother is required to acquiesce, to submit; the mother is to display the required parenting skills. Submitting to authority and engaging in a set series of therapeutic exercises were the basis for the tasks that are a service plan. They were also the ways workers judged whether a client 'is acting like a mother.' Finally, the service offered was counselling to understand and correct the neglect. This understanding of child abuse, according to the medical-psychological approach, has situated the pathology in the personality of the abusing mother. It presumed that neglect was a learned behaviour that only needed to be understood and corrected.

The second element of displaying behaviour appropriate enough to have children returned home was the quality of the weekly visit the parents were allowed with their children. 'The other thing is they monitor how often they visit, and supposedly the quality of the visit. I don't really know what that means. As long as they don't do anything real bad; it's hard to measure how good a quality a visit is' (Heenan, 2 June 1992).

The accomplishing of these lists of services, coupled with appropriate behaviour during the counselling sessions, was what workers believed clients did to play the game of being a client. For the mother who was motivated, for whatever reason, to play the game, retention or return of her children was possible. Some workers were cynical about any change of heart: 'I think a lot of people change their ways, not because of what they learn in counselling or in Parenting Skills classes but they say I don't want that son-of-a-bitch back in my face again' (Reid, 7 May 1992).

As parents began acting appropriately, they allowed themselves to be moulded into treatment-going, therapy-receiving, acquiescent people. The protection of children was accomplished through control of their parents. 'The father is going every week (to a private agency) and learning parenting skills and he spends almost all morning with his boy getting parenting skills by that agency' (Delval, 15 June 1992). Erica Kane speaks approvingly of a Chippewa family.

They've been saving money, they have an apartment, they've been buying a lot of furniture. They have all the physical things they need like beds, all the important things. They have a two bedroom apartment which is bigger than what they had before; they had a one bedroom before, that's were they had been living before with the kids. And they are in a treatment program for alcoholism, both of them. There was this prerequisite, that they had to go through seven or eight group meetings and if they went to all of those and didn't miss any of them, they could start individual sessions which they just started. I asked (father) what happened and he said well when she's not drinking it saves a lot of money. She's been to every visit (with the children), which she never did before, she was much more sporadic. If they're going (to the meetings) on a regular basis and if they are really participating, if they are using their time well, instead of just sitting there and wasting time, which I don't think they would do, the kids would be able to go home in the near future, maybe in a few months (Kane, 1 July 1992).

An important part of the social construction of being a successful client, therefore, and despite all the mandating and organising of counselling and classes, was the notion that it must be done on one's own. Erica Kane spoke about the same couple, 'when they decided they were going to go ahead and do something they went back to this other place so I didn't, myself, refer them to this agency but they remembered it' (Kane, 1 July 1992). The idea of self-help underlies much of the helping discourse about parents in child welfare practice.

Homogenising clients

In an attempt to see what differences workers saw among the different racial groups of clients, I had asked Arthur Reid how the court system saw Indian clients. The courts are only part of the child welfare system but they do play a pivotal role in the definition and management of child abuse and neglect. I was interested in seeing if Reid thought there was some sort of differentiation between Indian and non-Indian clients by the courts. He replied that, not only were Indian clients virtually ignored by the courts except for the legalities of the Indian Child Welfare Act, but that all clients were treated much the same. Reid's assertion was supported by DCFS workers at another Chicago office who told me that in working with Indians 'the only real difference was the need to document decisions more closely than for other groups' (Field notes, 19 September 1990). Reid told me,

I think they just see them as they see everybody else, just a mass. Some of those judges will see over a 100 cases a day. I don't think they even see the faces; its just a voice that's down below the bench. Some of them will look at the legal side. They'll ask you have you notified the tribal commission of this, that's the only thing they'll ask you. Say, 'Yes,' and that's it, that's the end of it. They don't discuss it. They just want to make sure that the legalities are observed. There's no separate justice in that sense, there's no recognition of cultural differences when you go in with an Indian case (Reid, 7 May 1992).

Thus, the sheer weight of numbers that confronted the courts tended to treat each case as a checklist of things to be done and the recipient of a standard set of services and expectations. The pressure by the courts to tell each case as an instance of a generic clientele was only partly resisted by workers. Much of their own practice, in their formulation of service plans, reflected the same procedures that they criticised in the courts. Indian cases, much as other racial groups, were all treated the same way and with the same services.

In a client's service plan, a series of tasks were set for each problem or objective identified by the worker. A reading of client service plans, a staple component of every case file, revealed that the goals for a case were expressed in almost identical terms. 'The record is not, therefore, a construction of past events; it is a practical construction of an approved reality' (Pithouse, 1987, p. 39). Arthur Reid called it boilerplating. The following example was taken from the file of a ten year old Menominee girl, sexually abused by her stepfather. The girl was placed with her aunt who had initially reported the sexual abuse to DCFS. The case worker was Arthur Reid.

Objective: to enable (girl) to benefit from association with the foster home.

Client and service tasks:

1. The relative foster mother will ensure that (girl) continues in counselling.
2. The foster mother will encourage and enable (girl) to participate in such activities as will enhance her emotional, physical and social development.
3. The foster mother shall provide all necessary food, shelter, clothing, and medical service.
4. The foster mother will report all unusual incidents to DCFS.
5. The foster mother will obtain DCFS authorization for all major medical service.
6. The foster mother will not allow (girl) to be in the presence of her mother without constant supervision. (Stepfather) will not be allowed access to (girl).
7. DCFS worker will explore daycare options with the foster mother.

Arthur Reid devised this plan for an Administrative Case Review which is an internal DCFS review of each case every six months to ensure that mandated guidelines were being kept. Administrative Case Reviews and courts are situations child welfare work becomes public and visible (Pithouse, 1987). During the review, Arthur turned to me and said, 'this sort of language is what you write for cases with a return-home goal.'

'Boilerplating,' then, is the written construction of the case as fulfilling the goals and behaviours required both by law and by what the workers consider 'appropriate' parenting or child behaviour to be. It is the written construction of the case according to a particular point in its career as a case. 'There's a great deal of (boilerplating) you know (laughs). Its the only way you can live with the paperwork. I have my way of saying it, I've said it for five years. Some reasons I'm fond of, I guess. That way I don't have to think about it. I say it the same way every damn time' (Reid, 7 May 1992). Workers' use of boilerplating produced a social construction of the client that homogenised all children into one generic client.

'It's all about documentation'

The production of paperwork about the client and the keeping of the resultant file was one of the central features of child welfare practice at City Office. Paperwork is essential for child welfare practice, as was evidenced by workers complaints when they received new cases with incomplete or missing paperwork. Paperwork was also a means of checking that the worker was managing the case according to departmental guidelines and that the various laws and regulations were being observed. The Administrative Case Review was created to monitor workers' compliance with laws and regulations. 'Now, you just fill out forms on people, over and over again. It seems all you do now is write and document things so you don't get in trouble and you never try to alleviate the problem that needs to be alleviated' (Heenan, 2 June 1992). Paperwork becomes more important than people work.

Documentation plays a central place in the construction of the 'facts' about clients in public welfare agencies (Hasenfeld, 1972; Zimmerman, 1969). The amount of paperwork required of child welfare workers has increased since the Adoption Assistance and Child Welfare Act of 1980 (Kamerman and Kahn, 1990). A primary source of documentation, which the caseworker must keep filed and up to date, is the series of formal transactions between child welfare, legal, medical, and other personnel involved in each case. Case records allow the workers to document and retain information about their clients (Kagle, 1984). 'It's all about documentation. So the faster you can bring in documentation, the faster you could return a kid home or close out the case in court. That's all they look at is the paperwork' (Taina Aponte, 28 May 1992). Documentation is also a way of holding workers accountable for the services and supervision they provide to their clients (Zimmerman, 1969).

Child welfare workers at City Office spent at least three days a week in the office calling clients and private agencies, recording notes on these conversations and filling in forms about their clients. Each case had to be reviewed by a DCFS Administrative Case Reviewer every six months and each case took at least a half day to prepare. Time spent on paperwork was time not spent with clients.

> The paperwork is horrendous, you really don't get to spend the time with the family that you should, go out and see them, get to know the kids the way you should. You come in, you spend 20 minutes and you're gone. I was involved with one case that had 14 kids in it. So to do a case review, one on each child, that was a killer. I come into work an hour early, there's nobody bothers me and the phone doesn't ring. Then I usually eat at my desk and work through, because right now I'm trying to get this stuff out of the way; there's a lot of catch-up to play' (Reid, 23 March 1992).

The emphasis in DCFS on paperwork over fieldwork structured what it meant to be a worker. While all the workers in this study shared the romantic ideology of the child welfare worker, the reality was that they must work as clerks. Time spent at their desks and time spent/wasted in Juvenile Court placed more value on the written construction of the case and less on the personal relationship with clients that workers' valued as being central to their work.

Child welfare practice at City Office was situated within legislation, rules of procedure, and the paperwork they generate. (This was a contrast to England where, when Pithouse (1987) did his research, personal experience seemed to be valued over following procedures). While the child welfare system created a supervisory regime over clients (Frost and Stein, 1989) embodied in the case file to monitor client performance, the same system also created a supervisory regime for workers. The bureaucratic emphasis on paperwork can, therefore, dominate the definition of what workers are employed for. In the following account, Bob Heenan spoke to the differing notions of his work held by his own department and by outsiders. DCFS' definition of child welfare worker centred around the workers' performance of bureaucratic tasks. Others saw the worker as an autonomous, even skilful, professional.

> From the administration's point of view, you are here to do the paperwork. I don't think they think workers need to be too brilliant to do that. (We're) more like mules. In other situations,

66

in the media or in court, you are looked on as some kind of all purpose expert in everything. You're supposed to be detective, doctor, lawyer, social worker, priest, magician, guru. Then when you come back to work, you are treated like a mule again (Heenan, 2 July 1992).

What was important to the department, then, according to this worker, were bureaucratic, not professional, skills. Close attention to bureaucratic tasks was safer for a department that was so often criticised in the media. '(DCFS) is run by, not the interest of what should be good for kids and families, but what is politically and legally safe' (Heenan, 2 July 1992).

Bureaucratic expectations produced bureaucratic responses. Workers worried about making sure that there was little chance of their being penalised for omitting to provide services to clients. 'To return a kid home I would have a letter signed by the therapist saying that they agree with that and why. So if something did go wrong, you know that would cover you as a caseworker' (Accardo, 20 March 1992). 'Because the department has had so many problems that it's wound up on the front page of the paper, everybody talks about cover your butt, just make sure you cover your butt' (Valdez, 14 May 1992).

Effort spent in covering workers' butts meant that children were more likely to be dealt with bureaucratically. As Janine Cooper said, 'To cover myself, I'll bring this case in (to court)' (Cooper, 12 May 1992). The fear that workers had about keeping their jobs, and the situations of stress and even harassment they met in Juvenile Court, lead them to apply the most restrictive solutions to problems they encountered with their clients. 'Investigators and workers, they always feel if you've got a situation and you have no real solution for it, take the children. Put them in foster care' (Valdez, 14 May 1992). This was more likely to happen when workers were rushed because of the large numbers of cases they had. In these circumstances, workers acted to defend themselves from possible censure. While this may also be construed as protecting children or servicing clients, the worker had become the focus of the intervention rather than the client.

The valuing of the worth and dignity of the individual, emphasised in client self-determination, shared goals of intervention, and help without domination, is an important aspect of practice (Bartlett, 1970). Yet, from the central computer of the Hotline to the boilerplate of the service plan, clients had been standardised and homogenised for greater efficiency. The erasure of the individual client had, at the same time, erased the professional competence of the child welfare worker. Bureaucratisation of practice had called into question the motivation and vision of workers who, initially, saw their work as having greater importance, for themselves as well as for children and families, than form filling and supervision. 'We're supposed to have the whole damn thing resolved in nine months, now. We're to come to the final solution in nine months. So we just go bang, bang, bang, bang (Reid, 23 March 1992). If 'needs talk' (Fraser, 1989) is a site of struggle, these child welfare workers were losing the struggle to lawyers and bureaucrats.

There was a further homogenisation of children and their families in the fiction of the intact family portrayed in the stereotypical view of clients' families as disrupted traditional families. This stereotype became visible in the same Administrative Case Review discussed above. Speaking about the 'return home' goal for the young girl, Arthur Reid and the Case Reviewer spoke of the girl's mother and father as if they were an intact family.

> Thus, in the new objectives and tasks, Arthur has written that 'the mother will behave appropriately.' Again, (the Case Reviewer) said, they 'have to say something' about the father… They set out behaviours for them to do, 'behave appropriately' for mother, 'visit monthly' for father. And this was so even though the child had not seen (father) since she was a baby, if then. They decided on monthly contact (for the father). (Case Reviewer) asked Arthur to conduct a diligent search for father (Field notes, 2 May 1992).

The construction of a stereotypical family in the service plan has sanctioned unrealistic roles for the girl's mother and father and unattainable goals for the worker. Wattenberg (1985) has also noted that mothers are often constructed as collaborators in the sexual assaults on their daughters. Such was the case here. Point 6 of the service plan, in the list of tasks for the foster mother, stated, 'The foster mother will not allow (girl) to be in the presence of her mother without constant supervision. (Stepfather) will not be allowed access to (girl).' Here, the mother was blamed for the violence of the step-father.

The stereotyping by an attorney of a mother as a collaborator in the sexual abuse of her daughter was the occasion for the resignation of one of the workers at City Office.

> Jane Accardo told me that (a worker) had been 'grilled' in court because the Guardian ad Litem had access to a psychological report that (the worker) hadn't got and the Guardian wanted to have the mother of a sexually abused girl receive more therapy before the girl could have an unsupervised visit. Apparently the Guardian was blaming the mother for not protecting the girl. The abuser is dying in hospital, so he is no threat. The 'grilling' had been so stressful for the worker she resigned from DCFS the next day (Field notes, 7 May 1992).

Dingwall et al. (1983) have noted that the perceived moral character of the parent is central to decision-making in child abuse and this is the case here. Stereotypically sexist views of mother's roles within a family reinforce the patriarchal imbalance of power in families (Wattenberg, 1985). Workers' acquiescence in these stereotypes, whether they agreed with them or not, not only disadvantaged the return of children to their families but created further unattainable case goals for workers.

Since an essential feature of the child welfare system is that 'victims' require 'perpetrators,' the sympathy and concern shown to children were not always extended to their parents.

> What's really wrong with the whole system is that the kids are punished for what the parents do, and the parents aren't punished at all. In fact, the parents are treated better than the average citizen because certain things are done for them, you know, rides are provided; they don't have to go and visit their kids, their kids are brought to them (Heenan, 2 June 1992).

Parents, because they were blamed, and legally charged, for the neglect or abuse of their child, were portrayed in negative and manipulative terms by the workers. As Pithouse (1987) has noted, the reasons workers have a cynical view of parents lie in the actual experience of child welfare work.

But experience was not the only teacher. As in the first child saving movement (Gordon, 1985), current child protection is a social construct that imposes particular standards of mothering and fathering children based on urban capitalism. Class and gender domination of child welfare clients continues through the use of the dominant values of the white, male, middle-class to reflect appropriate parenting and child welfare practice (Sarri and Finn, 1992). Arthur Reid has seen this attitude from child welfare workers. DCFS workers 'and private agency workers who've got an education, come off the North Shore and they want to take kids away' because 'the mother's put some mattresses on the floor and that's where the kids sleep' (Reid, 1 July 1992).

The privatisation of counselling and parenting services in Illinois can be articulated as the commodification of some women and their children. There was a continual taking of children from certain groups of mothers – the poor, minorities – to be given to other more morally deserving mothers who are paid by the state. The use of public agency child welfare workers as a conduit to private sector agencies that provide services for fees (Samantrai, 1991), or who receive contracts from the state to provide services, placed child welfare clients as commodities bought and sold in the marketplace (Sarri and Finn, 1992).

Silencing clients

An initial reaction by clients to DCFS involvement in their lives was fear. 'All the clients ever hear of the department is that DCFS takes children... With new assessment cases, it does take some time to formulate a relationship with the clients, obviously' (Valdez, 14 May 1992). DCFS was known as 'the baby snatchers' (Reid, 23 March 1992). Naturally, parents were not happy to have DCFS coming around to visit them. Parents did not see the involvement of DCFS workers from the same positive perspective of helping as the workers saw their work. If clients did want official help, they seemed to want material goods that they were not able to get for themselves. 'I don't think they see us as so much helping as I would like them to. We're really here to help them get their kids back. However, they see it in a different role. They want practical sort of stuff like money, housing, clothes' (Accardo, 19 May 1992).

Clients are silenced when they are treated as objects to be manipulated (Freire, 1985). The silencing of clients happened when workers convinced clients of their deviance before they could receive services. 'A lot of people aren't convinced that they are doing anything wrong, so part of the problem is to get them to realise that for their children's sake, they need to try some better ways of doing things' (Casey, 12 May 1992). Workers also silenced clients when they continued using stereotypical notions of families to guide their practice or when they created generic boilerplate for each of their cases. Above all, workers silenced clients when they insisted on clients doing what they were told, without argument.

Clients were also silenced when their wishes were ignored. Arthur Reid told of a Menominee family that wanted to handle an abusive situation itself. The family was re-defined as abusive.

> Initially I had quite a bit of resistance from the family; they wanted to handle it within the family and they attempted to do it. The mother gave the aunt a note when she went to court that said that she was giving her sister custody of this child. The family had the false assumption that if they did this they could bypass the court. The court just simply ignored it and took custody of the child at that time (Reid, 23 March 1992).

In this instance, the court ignored the family and constructed the child as 'officially' abused. The child was placed with the aunt but was now officially redefined as an abused child, with all the services and changes of status that entailed. The aunt was further redefined as a relative foster parent and had new responsibilities and supervision by a caseworker that were not hers as a mere aunt. While for many children and many families such a change of status may well be justified, not all clients readily accepted their redefinition.

The traditional performance of the courtroom, where attorneys spoke to each other and clients and workers only spoke if spoken to, was a site that silenced both parents and workers. Jane Accardo was conscious of the silencing of children in these situations: 'they're passed over way too much in the way we're working it now.' Parents, and children, 'just stand there.'

A lot of times (children are) not asked what's going on and they don't have any choice or say in the situation, even when they really can, I think, at certain ages they are able to say what they want. And for the best interests of the child, it really is passed over to somebody else who depends on their (own) opinion, what's the best interest.

Silencing of clients was especially evident when an attorney's opinion was based on 'ten minutes talking to lawyers about something and they just spit out whatever they feel like saying in your conversation is not good representation.' Accardo's solution is more dialogic, more interactional, more empowering.

I think I'd like to see us have more just hearings, sitting down at a table and talking with people and having a little more time. Sometimes you just need to sit down and all brainstorm what would be the best for this kid and for everybody's opinion, then we can come up with something more positive than the 'quick, hurry up, lets do this, do that' and 'here, this is what we expect' (Accardo, 30 June 1992).

Adult clients in child welfare practice were usually portrayed as passive people who need to be educated about how to look after and bring up their children. In fact, however, clients often did not accept this redefinition of themselves. As David Casey said, 'A lot of people aren't convinced that they are doing anything wrong' (Casey, 12 May 1992). Juan Valdez had found the same thing. Working mainly with Mexican families, he noted that, 'I see that with a lot of them they only did what they thought was right' (Valdez, 22 June 1992). Bob Heenan, too, had mentioned how some clients 'want to argue over and over' about whether they were good parents or not (Heenan, 22 June 1992).

Commentators view public child welfare clients as highly resistant of workers (Samantrai, 1991; Siu and Hogan, 1989a, 1989b). For Native American parents, for example, resistance may often take the form of avoidance. This could either be physical avoidance of the worker or avoidance of saying anything that would make the worker upset. The first placed the parents in the position of being non-cooperative and therefore more likely to have their children removed. The second was often construed as lying, manipulation, or indifference.

Six of the eight workers in this study gave accounts of resistance by Indian parents or adult relatives to the perceived interference of DCFS into their family life. Speaking of one of his Indian cases, Arthur Reid said, 'we don't know where they are at, they make no effort to contact us, we can't find them. [The parents] know where the children are, however, and they do come by occasionally to see the children' (Reid, 23 March 1992). He had asked an Indian colleague in Montana about a family who had lied to him.

'She said, 'They're not really lying, its a subject peoples' adaptation to their conqueror. They're just adjusting.' It's the passive resistance, they'll tell you exactly what you want to hear at the time and they walk away and they've forgotten it entirely. They have their own way of resisting (Reid, 7 May 1992). Whatever the reason, and however Native American and other clients explained it to themselves, workers saw their behaviour as manipulative and a rejection of the workers' assistance.

When it comes to child protection, follow-up workers are there to work with parents to keep their children with them or to get them back from foster parents. Parents' questioning of the competence of the worker to be able to give them advice on how to be a parent was also part of the resistance shown by clients Thus, while clients 'are pretty cooperative for the most part' (Accardo, 20 March 1992), they were also ready to challenge workers about their competence in advising them how to rear their children.

I don't have kids so a lot of parents won't listen to what I say.
I say to them, you don't have to have kids to know about them.
And they'll say, if you don't have kids, you just don't know,
you don't know. I don't know if they totally mean it. On our
team there's only one worker, Arthur's the only one with a kid,
and he's only got one (Heenan, 22 June 1992).

Parents' challenge of workers' competence was a further rejection of themselves as passive, acquiescent people. In resisting their redefinition, they challenged the power of DCFS and the courts to cast them in the role of abusing and neglectful parents. Their challenge, however, was always within an imbalance of power that worked to their disadvantage.

A further method of rejecting the official definition of themselves as abusing and neglectful parents, was playing the game of learning to be a good parent to convince a counsellor or therapist. In addition, workers believed clients shared knowledge about how to get the most out of their relationship with DCFS. "Clients have their own body of knowledge. They sit around that waiting room when they go in and they say, 'Well, you can tell him this, you can tell him that. Tell him you don't have bus fare, there's no way you can get there you don't have bus fare'" (Reid, 7 May 1992).

Different workers gave accounts of their anger at being, as they called it, manipulated by clients. 'It's so aggravating,' Jane Accardo told me as we left Juvenile Court to visit a Kiowa mother who had promised a number of times to be present with her baby. 'I know I'm going to take that kid. I don't know why I do this,' meaning keep him at home with his mother (Field notes, 21 April 1992). Parents who did not do what they were told breached the acceptable behaviour that workers wanted to see in a client. Parents' resistance could have grave consequences for their children because it gave cause for a worker to remove a child from the home. Even so, many mothers, many parents, resisted rather than acquiesced in the redefinition of themselves as bad parents.

Thus, the workers' perceptions of themselves as saving children was further challenged when they worked with the parents of their child-clients. Parents' resistance and challenge and the time workers spend in bureaucratic tasks rather than actually working with clients further challenges the official interpretation of child welfare as the protection of children. The main thesis of the following chapter is that, while child welfare work is inherently stressful, the work of the eight workers was made more stressful by the way the work was carried out and the context in which it took place. There was a fear in workers that their work would break and shatter them. Their own stress and personal trauma mirrored the disintegration within the child welfare system.

6 'It's no bed of roses'

In the sixteen months I visited City Office, I noticed a pronounced change in the atmosphere of the office. My early fieldnotes remarked on the busyness of the place, the workers talking together, the atmosphere of purposeful camaraderie. Later notes revealed a more sombre tone. '(There is) a difference in atmosphere at City Office between when I went there in 1991 and now. Now, it's grim. Before, it was more relaxed, pleasant, (workers) talking together. Now, it's quieter, grimmer, people working alone in their offices' (Field notes, 21 May 1992).

Stress is part of the job for child welfare workers, but it takes a variety of forms. There is the stress of working with involuntary clients within organisations which portray child welfare practice in narrow bureaucratic terms. There is the stress of working with children who have been abused and neglected. There is the personal danger of visiting dangerous neighbourhoods. Finally, there is the stress of too much work from growing caseloads. This chapter will consider each of these stressors in turn and relate their impact on practice.

In March 1992, David Casey told me morale was low, the lowest it had been. By May, a number of workers were saying the same thing. Arthur Reid told me his team had gone from eleven workers to five in the eleven months since he arrived at City Office (Field notes, 12 May 1992). One of those who had left was a worker who told me court work was 'gruelling' and that it was giving her headaches and 'physical problems' (Field notes, 6 May 1992). For the remaining workers, the strain of too many cases and too few workers began to show. Erica Kane remarked on the state of her desk, messily piled high with paper, forms, and files, as a sign of the overwhelming nature of the work she was doing. She said Fran, a colleague from the same team, had just returned from her honeymoon. Fran had called to say the honeymoon was very relaxing but last night she had had a nightmare about one of her clients. The same day, Bob Heenan told me that all the changes happening in DCFS and all the new cases he would be getting had made him too depressed to work (Field notes, 13 May 1992).

It might be thought that this was unusual, that overworking child welfare workers was only a sporadic occurrence and that I just happened to be there at a time when such a rare occurrence occurred. This is not so. Fryer et al. (1988) have noted that child protection workers generally are seriously overworked. In Illinois, according to Stehno (1990, p. 558), child welfare workers were 'increasingly overworked, underpaid, and unsupported.' She stated that the average DCFS worker had a caseload of over 60 and that caseloads as high as 80 were not uncommon. By the end of my research, the average caseload of the eight workers in this study was 62 cases. The Child Welfare League of America recommends a caseload of 20. Consequently, workers found it difficult to do effective case management as they spent most of their time responding to crises.

Stress and child welfare work

Child welfare work differs markedly from the idealised worker-client relationship of the voluntary therapeutic encounter (Seabury, 1985). Working with involuntary clients in child welfare raises moral dilemmas around the use of coercive power, the basic contradiction between the helping and investigative roles, balancing the rights of children, parents, foster parents and others, and managing the flow of confidential information (Siu and Hogan, 1989b). Furthermore, 'the ambiguity in existing definitions provides insufficient guidance to child welfare workers for such case management activities' (Hutchison, 1990, p. 63).

Stress may be accentuated when the workers become emotionally involved in rescuing the child or the parent from untenable living conditions (Samantrai, 1991). Allied with the dangers to children in untenable living conditions are physical and life-threatening dangers to workers who must visit children and parents as an integral part of their work. The risk of attack while visiting clients' homes, whether from the client or from unknown assailants, is rarely mentioned in the literature despite newspaper reports (Steinberg, 1991) about the dangerous neighbourhoods workers visit.

Besides stress from clients, the major source of stress on child welfare workers is the bureaucratic organisations in which they work (Barrett and McKelvey, 1980). Being overworked, underpaid, and unsupported (Stehno, 1990) are symptoms of the subordination of the workers to the organisational structure. The result is burnout, the combination of mental, psychological, and physical symptoms characterised by negativism, cynicism, inflexibility concerning rules, and blaming the victim (Arches, 1985). Workers lament that they cannot make a difference (Hartman, 1991).

Nationally, child protection workers are seriously overworked and their caseloads are huge and unmanageable (Fryer, Miyoshi and Thomas, 1989). In a no-longer atypical example, a report by the American Civil Liberties Union of Illinois charged that 'overburdened' DCFS caseworkers are actually abusing and neglecting children by not being able to provide the range of services children need (Cuadros, 1991).

Stress and burnout among child protection workers have been widely examined. Solutions often focus on individual or group treatment to relieve stress. This may be helpful to some individuals but workplaces can produce stress no matter how much or how little work people have. When cast as a personal issue, burnout camouflages collective and structural issues that need to be addressed (Esposito and Fine, 1985). Karger (1981) suggested using the term 'alienation' to focus on the objective and organisational aspects of stress. His analysis is helpful but it needs to recognise the contradictions inherent in the nature of child welfare practice that produce stress over and above the issue of too much work or a bad organisational environment (Esposito and Fine, 1985).

Child welfare practice is ambivalent work. It requires workers to constantly juggle competing understandings of what their purpose is. The tension between protecting children and keeping families together is at the heart of the paradox of child welfare policies (Jimenez, 1990). Jane Accardo made reference to that ambivalence: 'I think our job is confusing to me because a lot of times it's to ensure these children are in a safe place. However, at the same time, it's conflicting with trying to help moms and dads get better, also. It seems to me like it's two different jobs sometimes' (Accardo, 19 May 1992). The ambivalence of dealing with two different working worlds, the children as well as 'the moms and dads,' is also highlighted by the realisation that doing one's job creates stress and trauma for the children one is working to protect.

> The whole basic premise of this job is a no-win situation. If you remove the child from the family you are doing something that's going to effect his life forever or if you leave him in a bad situation that's also a horrible thing so you are trying to pick one of two arrangements, neither of which are very good (Casey, 22 November 1991).

Even when a worker has decided what needs to be done, the decision still places workers in a bind.

> The workers in the department are always kind of in a position where you're damned if you do and damned if you don't. (One supervisor) has a caricature of a man that's strung up on a tree getting ready to be hung and there's an angry mob and

underneath it says, 'social worker that allows a child to remain in an abusive home.' And then in the next caricature, it says, 'Social worker that removed a child from his parents,' and it has the same picture. You're damned if you do and you're damned if you don't. And with workers, it's a lot of stress. It's very difficult to make that decision (Valdez, 14 May 1992).

Two of the other seven workers had the same cartoon pinned above their desks. As David Casey noted, 'We have to juggle all these and try to make sense (of them), and get everybody headed in the same direction' (Casey, 22 November 1991). Much of child welfare work is negotiating so that everybody will head in the same direction. Time after time, I saw workers negotiate and bargain with clients, with attorneys, and with other child welfare professionals to accomplish agreed-on tasks and goals. Sometimes, there was a fine line between negotiating with people and telling them what to do. 'I think you need to find this fine line because you want to be able to have some control in the family's life but not too much because you want them to be able to take control of their own lives' (Kane, 15 June 1992).

Finding that fine line was not always easy. Two workers told me that only about 20% of cases were clear cut, where either the mother does all that is required of her or disappears altogether (Field notes, 13 May 1992). The remaining cases were the ones that had to be negotiated through. It was in these cases, as Pithouse (1987, p. 8) has asserted, that 'the uncertain outcomes of social work intervention can have potentially demoralising effects upon practitioners.'

There was a further source of stress for the worker. Working with maltreated children is stressful in itself. 'Basically (stress) comes from the fact that we are dealing every day with children that are being mistreated' (Casey, 22 November 1991). Working with some clients was especially stressful and some workers cannot do it. On a field visit with Arthur Reid, I noted, "Back at the car, after visiting a mother and child with AIDS, Arthur said, 'She's going to die, the kid is going to die, the boyfriend's going to die. It's strange working with people you know are going to die. Some workers won't do it'" (Field notes, 10 June 1992).

Child welfare work means having to take hard decisions about issues that directly effect the lives of children and their families. It is a stressful job that is valued by workers for the importance it means to children. The complexity and problematic nature of child welfare work may go some way to explaining the negative, and even contradictory, feelings of workers about their work. When the innate stress of their work was added to the context of blame and scapegoating of DCFS workers current in Chicago at the time of the research, pressure and stress on the workers increased.

There's also a lot of pressures on the workers. If something happens, the workers are blamed a lot for things that are

77

beyond their control. Nobody likes that, nobody likes that at all. Some people bring it on themselves, but also there's a lot of blame going around (and) placed on workers who are really overworked, not given enough tools to do the job that needs to be done (Casey, 22 November 1991).

A variety of stresses, therefore, are an inherent part of the job, created by the need to the juggle the responsibilities of protecting children and of keeping families together and of working with children who have been abused and neglected. However, there were stresses that were not inherent in child welfare practice itself but arose from the way the practice was carried out. Consider Erica Kane's summary of what she disliked about her work.

I think I would much prefer doing this kind of job if we didn't have to go to court all the time and didn't have to deal with the judges and the attorneys that yell at you. If we had fewer families to work with we could spend more time with them and do a better job. I don't feel like I put in enough time with the actual people to really make a difference to them. And, you know, some of this paperwork too, if some of this paperwork could be alleviated that would be a big help as well (Kane, 1 July 1992).

The rest of this chapter will consider two external sources of stress for child welfare workers at City Office, court work and threats to them of danger and violence.

The legal-isation of child welfare practice

Commentators make a claim that child welfare work has been medicalised. Child welfare practice, however, offers as much evidence of its legal-isation. At each stage of the career of a case, there are a series of court hearings. These include an emergency placement hearing when the initial report of abuse or neglect report is substantiated, a fact-finding hearing to decide the facts in the case, a disposition hearing to decide where the child will be placed, and a series of judicial oversight hearings while the child is in care. Finally, if the child is placed for adoption, there are lengthy hearings to dissolve parental rights (Hardin, 1990).

Attending Juvenile Court was a major source of external stress and aggravation to workers. When I asked Arthur Reid how he would explain his work to other people, he immediately focussed on the Juvenile Court and the ways in which judges and attorneys shaped the discourse and practice of child welfare work.

Well, it's no bed of roses. You are going to be disappointed as
hell; you're going to be frustrated by the courts who will not
take custody when you are convinced that the child is in
danger... you know a lot but you can't put everything in
evidence in front of a court . . . (On the other hand), there were
times you'd get kids whom you don't feel should ever have
been in the system (Reid, 7 May 1992).

The Juvenile Court building was a dark, five storey fortress on South
Hamilton Street, Chicago. Each visitor was screened by metal detectors and
armed deputies patrolled the corridors. The courtrooms, called Calendars,
and their waiting rooms were arranged so that each particular Calendar
heard cases from a different geographical area of the city. This account is
from one of the many visits I made to Juvenile Court.

The waiting room walls are greyish brick, without windows or
pictures or posters. People sit side by side on long, black
benches. The clients waiting are mainly African-American; the
service people mainly white. Most of the time the noise is very
loud; there are people talking over each other, children yelling
or crying. Periodically someone comes out of the courts and
yells out a name; this is the signal for a group of people to get
up and go in for their hearing.

When called, you go through the large, darkened glass door to
the court. At the back of the court are three long benches like
the ones outside. To the right is a small table covered with
children's books and two small chairs for children. In front of
the table is the desk where the three States Attorneys sit. On
the opposite side of the court to the States Attorneys, in front
of the benches, sit the Public Defenders and the Guardians ad
Litem. Across the end of the court is the raised judge's bench
with a sign that names the judge presiding (Field notes, 4 June
1992).

The noisy, seemingly chaotic atmosphere of the court waiting rooms and
then the hushed tenseness of the hearing was intimidating. 'Court is the
tensest time when someone's new. (Workers) go in there and they're
terrified. You see people down there trembling when they go in front of that
court. You have judges that will just rip you to pieces and some of the
attorneys will do the same' (Reid, 1 July 1992).

Compounding the atmosphere of the courtroom was the negative
opinions some judges had of DCFS workers. 'I know a lot of them (judges)
in there are pretty hostile towards us. They have negative views, they think
we're not doing all we're supposed to do' (Casey, 12 May 1992). Some
judges were not loathe to share their negative views – 'I've heard the judge,
in between cases, gossip about the DCFS workers, about how they're all

alike, they never do this, they never do that' (Cooper, 12 May 1992). This attitude was sometimes shared by attorneys. 'There's some attorneys that kind of talk down to you' (Kane, 15 June 1992). One judge, in particular, had taken it upon himself to discipline DCFS workers. He had a Roladex address book on his bench to identify workers who had missed or been late for a court date. He also had Monday afternoon 'spanking sessions' for workers who had been late or had missed court (Cooper, 12 May 1992). This practice was reported in the *Chicago Sun-Times* (Baldacci, 1992). (The newspaper article was pinned to a notice board on the third floor at City Office. DCFS staff were avid readers of newspaper stories about their department). However, as Arlinda Delval said, "He has bad temper with everybody. Even the lawyers in his Calendar alert the workers, 'Be careful, he is not in a good mood, today'" (Delval, 15 June 1992).

While the way judges, and attorneys, treated workers added to the amount of stress in workers' lives, the prerogative of the judges to decide and shape child welfare practice constituted the legalisation of child welfare practice. The denigration and powerlessness of the workers before the court made clearer the hierarchy of power in child welfare. The very court setting reproduced in dramaturgical form the legal control of child welfare work. The judge was set above the people, seated, while the attorneys, workers and clients stood. Workers and clients could only speak if spoken to. Deference, compliance, and passivity were all valued there. 'The judge has returned kids home when I didn't feel it was appropriate, but that wasn't anything that I, or the (DCFS) attorneys, felt that we should appeal' (Kane, 20 March 1992). There was an ironic parallel in the way the court treated those before it and the way workers expected clients to behave.

The identification of those who had the real power in child welfare practice, judges and attorneys, comes through in the following statement from Juan Valdez. He was explaining to me how DCFS was blamed for decisions that were not its fault. 'It was the judge and the attorneys that had this discussion and it was the judge that approved it and, of course, the judge's name doesn't get mentioned, it's the department' (Valdez, 14 May 1992). Bob Heenan was quite explicit, 'In court, you have to do what they say' (Heenan, 2 June 1992).

Doing what 'they' say was a source of aggravation to workers who did not have high opinions of some of the judges and attorneys. Most of the workers I interviewed thought the attorneys were young and inexperienced. They contrasted their own sense of purpose with the opportunism they ascribed to court officials. Workers believed attorneys and judges did not want to be in Juvenile Court and were only using the position as a stepping stone to better things. 'Juvenile Court is the starting ground for most of the states' attorneys and public defenders (before) they are promoted to higher courts' (Casey, 22 November 1991).

These are brand new lawyers. You are telling them a lot of
things that they are supposed to be doing. It doesn't make
much sense; too many cases, too many people, new lawyers,
no one wants to be there. You can see the judges; they don't
want to be there. It seems like children are the last priority . . .
You know the gossip is that a certain judge wants out. Actually
one specific judge will get up on the bench and tell you that
(Accardo, 20 March 1992).

Overall, these workers felt that it was the court that controlled child
welfare practice. 'There's a lot of things controlling DCFS. You have the
laws, the court, outside forces, the media to a certain extent' (Kane, 15 June
1992). Partly, this is because court officials and child welfare workers have
different understandings of child welfare practice. Geiser (1973) believed
that child welfare workers and courts talk a different language in regard to
child welfare. He said workers focus on current and future needs of
children and on parental failure to meet those needs while courts focus on
legally admissible evidence and clear and present dangers to children.
Feminist writers have identified the patriarchally constructed inequality of
the current court system. "Lynne Spender, lecturer in feminist
jurisprudence at the University of Technology (Sydney, Australia) regards
the adversarial process which 'pits lawyer against lawyer in a competitive,
winner-and-loser, egoistic, public battle' as a flawed, masculine way to
arrive at justice" (Cummings, 1992).

Differing agendas for protecting children, coupled with what workers
saw as the unequal exercise of legal power, served to underline a significant
source of stress for child welfare workers. This became apparent in the
uncertainty surrounding one of David Casey's cases. A young Stockbridge-
Munsee woman had given birth to her fourth child who had tested positive
for cocaine. Her other three children were fostered with relatives. David
Casey and the child protection investigator had recommended that the baby
stay with the mother. The Guardian ad Litem was vigorously opposing this
and Casey was caught between what he thought was best for the child and
what the Guardian thought was best. In the adversarial arena of the
courtroom, there was more than the child's best interests at stake. The
mother's history of child care and long-standing criticism of DCFS workers
by the judge hearing the case made Casey feel that his professional
judgement and reputation, even his job, were also under threat. The
following account of the court hearing plays out the day-to-day tensions
inherent in child welfare practice.

It is Tuesday morning at Juvenile Court. No one seems too sure
what to do. The mother has been ordered by the court to take
a drug evaluation on the previous Friday. Casey has checked.
She did not take the evaluation and she is not in court. The

Public Defender wants to know if there's anything new. Casey tells him about the missed drug evaluation. He looks worried, tense. He is afraid the Guardian ad Litem will accuse him of not protecting the baby.

The Guardian ad Litem was unsure, too. She asks Casey what she should do. Casey is ambivalent; he doesn't give a direct opinion. The Guardian has been given a second-hand report that there was domestic violence on the mother by the father. Casey is surprised. He says he hasn't heard of it. He disclaims any sure knowledge, 'It could be right. I don't know.' Both now look worried, serious. After the Guardian goes away, Casey turns to me and says, 'She's (Guardian) alright. She's not a ball-buster. Maybe, she's right, I don't know. The mother's already fucked up her first chance (the drug evaluation). At least, I can go to bed thinking I gave her a chance (Field notes, 23 June 1992).

The mother eventually came late to court, with the baby, and stated that she had taken the drug evaluation on Monday, the day before the court hearing. Casey told me that this could be a ploy to ensure that a drug-free weekend would result in a clean evaluation. During the hearing, the judge showed his annoyance with the Guardian by openly doubting the competence of the Guardian's witness (to the mother's lack of parenting skills) and by advising the Guardian on how to conduct her case. In the end, the judge left the child with her mother. He placed responsibility for the child's continued safety with Casey, ordering him, 'Mr Casey, if the child is at risk or the mother doesn't comply, file a supplemental or take Protective Custody' (Field notes, 23 June 1992).

The strain on Casey during this hearing became evident outside the courtroom. The mother asked Casey for money for the bus fare home. He was furious and loudly stated that he had given her enough in the past. He refused to give her any money. As we walked out to his car, he told me he was frustrated with the mother and angry at the father for sending her to Juvenile Court without money. I remarked that the judge, who had a reputation for verbally attacking DCFS workers, seemed to have come down on his side in this case. Casey retorted, 'What a bullshitter. Because he's attacking the Guardian, he's friendly to me; if he's attacking DCFS, he's friendly to the Guardian' (Field notes, 23 June 1992).

In this account, Casey was experiencing the usual juggling between uncertain outcomes that is common in child welfare practice. He had recommended the child stay with the mother yet he was not completely sure that this was the right decision. The eventual 'rightness' of his decision was tied closely with what happened to the child in its mother's care and on the mother cooperating with the provisions of the Protective Order. Part of his uncertainty, and possibly his frustration, was his knowledge of her noncooperation in the past. Exactly twelve months before, after the third child was removed, David Casey had written in the case file: 'Mother's attendance at drug counselling and parenting skills classes has been sporadic' (File note, 24 June 1991). A year before that, the private agency where the mother went for counselling after the first two children were indicated for neglect was more specific:

> (Mother) repeatedly expressed her feelings that substance abuse counselling was an unnecessary and unfair demand on her time and her attitude throughout the course of treatment was one of thinly veiled hostility towards this worker as well as apparent contempt for the whole treatment intervention process. (Mother) admitted that she was attending solely to comply with the court mandate (Report in case file, dated 19 June 1990).

Casey's decision to support the mother in keeping her child appeared to be based on a long professional relationship with her that led him to believe that she would not deliberately harm the baby. (By the time of this court hearing the baby had been safely with the mother for one month). Casey spoke disdainfully to me outside the court about evidence that the mother didn't know how to hold the baby, noting that she had sat in the waiting room for hours and then had stood before the judge, all the while holding the baby properly. I wrote in my notebook, 'His attitude to (the mother) is ambivalent. She frustrates and angers him yet he is scornful of people who criticise her' (Field notes, 23 June 1992).

There are a number of elements in this account that are pertinent to varying understandings of child welfare work by practitioners and by legal officials. First, the worker and the client built an interactive relationship over time and it was not the objective, rational stance of the emotionally uninvolved professional. In this context, Dingwall et al. (1983) have emphasised that child protection raises complex moral and political issues which have no one right technical solution. Yet, court decisions presumed that technical solutions were sufficient. In the case detailed above, besides saying what the mother had to do, the Protective Order spelt out formally the DCFS caseworkers' responsibilities. It was apparent that the Juvenile Court had its own form of boilerplating: the Order of Protection was a pro-forma document. There were 14 sections on the Order. Sections 10 and 13 were directed at DCFS. Section 10 was in bold print and was underlined: 'DCFS or its assigns shall schedule the first drug screen within 14 days of the writing of this order.' Casey had done this, although the mother had not complied with the proviso that she have the drug screen within 36 hours of being notified. Section 13 was in bold type with some underlining: 'DCFS or its assigns shall have in place all services required per this Order within

30 days of the entry of this Order' (Field notes, 23 June 1992). The legal requirements made of DCFS were standard for each Order. The judge had added three further sections to the pro-forma document: parenting skills class for the mother; father to be present at next court hearing; DCFS to notify the court immediately of a positive drug test.

Second, each worker was held accountable by the court for deciding if the child was safe, or not, and whether to remove the child, or not. The exercise of the worker's judgement had risks for the child, the mother, and for the worker her/himself. Third, the making of that judgement took place within an adversarial context, the court, where the worker could only respond to questions and not initiate discussion or argument. This was a position of powerlessness for the worker, where the worker had to accept a passive stance. In this the worker became like the client; both must passively await the questions and interrogations of the attorneys and the judge. Thus, stresses on the workers came not only from worry about their own judgements about clients. These stresses were compounded in the adversarial climate of the court.

Danger and violence

The possibility of violence was a constantly present threat to workers when they had to visit families living in dangerous neighbourhoods. Some workers had had little experience of violence – 'there's been a couple of things here and there but nothing that I felt was an actual threat on my life or my health or anything' (Kane, 25 June 1992). Even so, 'We get verbal assaults all the time, especially in court when the parents have already had the children removed. We are threatened, routinely, basically verbal threats that they are going to get you or kill you. Most of the people that are doing that are mentally ill and you have to realise where they are coming from' (Casey, 22 November 1991).

Some assaults are physical. Arthur Reid had had his car vandalised. Others, Janine Cooper and David Casey, had been assaulted.

> I've had experiences where I've been assaulted on the job and this was at one particular housing project which are generally very dangerous places. I had been going to this one for a year and a half and nobody had ever bothered me. I felt like I'd left my guard down one time and I got jumped by three teenagers. They just jumped on me, knocked me down and kicked me around a little. They never said a word, not one word. That's the only time in seven years I have been physically assaulted. I think that most of the people know who we are and what we are trying to do (Casey, 22 November 1991).

Within City Office's jurisdiction was Riverside Meadows (pseudonym), a housing project for the Chicago Housing Authority. Thousands of poor African-Americans lived in a sprawling complex of ten and 15 storey highrises. It was a dangerous place. Shootings were common and workers felt very apprehensive about going there. I had the same feelings when I accompanied a worker for a series of visits.

> We stopped well outside the complex and Gail put her purse in the trunk. She did this outside so that no one would see her do it. She remarked, 'Casework shouldn't have to be like this.' Both Gail and I were fairly tense during our time in Riverside Meadows. She appeared tight-lipped, focused, and walked quickly. I noticed that I was sweating a bit. I also noticed that my shoulders relaxed when we finally drove out (Field notes, 16 June 1992).

Despite the danger, workers still have to visit clients wherever they live. During the course of the research, a 15 year old girl was shot by a sniper in a Chicago Housing Project near City Office at 5 o'clock in the evening (Silverman, 1992). Yet, as one supervisor said to his staff at a team meeting, 'We can't not service people because they live in a dangerous area' (Field notes, 28 May 1992). Workers usually visited dangerous areas alone and they had developed a number of precautions to ensure their safety.

> The first step is probably just the neighbourhood itself. Driving up and wondering about the safety of the neighbourhood. You can tell in a minute, you know, whether you want to leave your car out front or not. They always say you can take the police but, sometimes, that would be more dangerous to go in with a police officer. Usually I will go really early in the morning, about eight or nine o'clock, when the kids are going to school so there are a lot of kids going in and out. Usually people are sleeping at that point. Really, even past ten in the morning, once they start getting up, forget it. It's not worth it, to my mind. I have done field work a lot and, at first, I thought it was kind of neat. I wanted to see these things but I don't think it is neat anymore. You will hear on the news, like from six o'clock on, people are literally shooting each other. So a lot of times I question how they can expect case workers to go out and do this kind of work (Accardo, 20 March 1992).

Like Jane Accardo, other workers had learned to take preventive action to minimise the risk of going to dangerous neighbourhoods. Arthur Reid wore police shoes. He said people saw the shoes and gave him a wide berth. Other workers dressed down, by wearing nondescript clothes, before entering poor neighbourhoods. They removed jewellery and stashed purses and bags in the trunk of their cars. Workers knew they had to visit dangerous neighbourhoods every week, so they went prepared.

The other thing is you just go in like you belong there; you know where you're going and you don't dally, you don't spend all your time looking over your shoulder like you're frightened. They notice all of those things. You get on the elevator with the kids and you kid with them and you do that. Sometimes, I'll put some peppermints in my pocket and hand them out to little kids in the elevator and that always seems to help. I had an old lady stop me once when I was going into this building and she said to me, 'everybody knows what you're doing here, don't come in the same way every time.' So from that time on I did what she said (Reid, 23 March 1992).

Other workers were not so gregarious. The worker I accompanied to Riverside Meadows did not talk to people in the elevators, wasted little time on pleasantries with clients, and left the housing project as quickly as she could. We spent 90 minutes in the whole complex, visited six apartments, spending eleven and 13 minutes respectively with the only two families that were in, and we moved quickly and purposefully (Field notes, 16 June 1992).

Visiting clients in their own homes was one method of working that set DCFS workers apart from private agency workers. Private agency workers usually had clients come to see them while DCFS workers usually visited clients in their homes. To meet a private agency worker, as Arlinda Delval recounted of a Menominee parent who was looking for work after an industrial accident, a client must attend an office or institutional setting. 'The father is going every week to (a private agency) and learning parenting skills and he spends almost all morning with his boy getting parenting skills by that agency' (Delval, 15 June 1992). Learning for father and child took place in an unfamiliar environment. In contrast and despite the threat of danger, DCFS workers visited clients in their own homes.

Why, then, with all this stress and disappointment, do workers stay on in their jobs? The next chapter shows how the stress of their work impacts on them, what they do about it and why many of them stay.

7 Working in child welfare

The main topics of conversation around City Office towards the end of this research were increasing caseloads and their effect on workers. More children being indicated as abused and neglected coupled with the resignation or transfer of workers meant higher caseloads for those workers remaining. Bob Heenan had 14 new cases waiting for him on his desk when he returned from vacation. At that time, each of the workers in his team had received at least nine new cases because two workers had transferred (Field notes, 22 March 1992). This began to have a multiplier effect and workers began to leave, thereby creating even greater caseloads for those remaining. Heenan's supervisor was well aware of the extra pressures the growth in cases placed on workers even as she was powerless to do anything about it.

> (She) says workers are leaving because of the large numbers of new cases. She says that now it's more than a body can bear. Normally, with a full complement of staff, they'd have about 45 cases. Now it's up to 80. By 1993 (because of reforms), it's supposed to be (down to) 25. Experienced staff are transferring to places where they don't have to manage cases; staff who haven't got the seniority to transfer are resigning. She thinks she'll get new staff from other Area Offices who'll think it's fine to have only 80 cases (Field notes, 4 June 1992).

Workers' dismay at the increase in cases and the subsequent increased pressure on themselves could be tangible at times. "Ten minutes after the supervisor spoke to me, Bob Heenan yelled out from his office, after reading his messages, 'Oh, God, she had twins, goddamn bitch. Last week I hear she's pregnant and now she has twins.' He turns to me and says, 'She's got four other kids in placement; anyone who's got four in placement can have six'" (Field notes, 4 June 1992). More cases meant more supervision of clients and extra work making sure that each case was correctly identified and serviced. At the same time, with more and more children being indicated as abused and neglected, DCFS wanted workers to move cases quickly through the system (Accardo, 20 March 1992).

> A lot of (cases) are in pretty bad shape. It's more work than working with a new case where you know what you don't have. (New cases have) got bombshells; you come along and you suddenly find something's missing. I've literally had cases come to me and its nothing but a folder with a name on it, and there's nothing there to tell me where they live or anything else. You don't get too many of them but I've got two of them here. (He points to two files). Those are probably the ones that if you don't get out on them right away they will blow up in your face. (He points to another file). This is one of the new ones we just got. This one's come from another unit. We were first involved in that in September, I can't find any contact at all since then (Reid, 23 March 1992).

Responsibility for a case implied to those outside DCFS that having a child welfare worker involved was enough. Jane Accardo disagreed, 'I think that it is just an impossible job and people in society expect everything to just roll along perfectly' (Accardo, 19 May 1992). For workers, having more cases meant a greater chance of being blamed for something that goes wrong, whether it was their responsibility or not.

> There's a lot of pressures on the workers. If something happens, the workers are blamed for a lot of things that are beyond their control. Nobody likes that, nobody likes that at all. Some people bring it on themselves, but also there's a lot of blame going around, placed on workers who are really overworked, and not given enough tools to do the job that needs to be done (Casey, 22 November 1991).

Having more cases also meant spending more time in the office doing paperwork and less time visiting clients. Asked to give an example of being overworked, David Casey told me,

> We are just assigned to monitor too many families. You can't get out and see these people as much as you can and you are making judgements basically on what you know, and if you haven't seen them enough you can't make that good of a judgment (Casey, 22 November 1991).

Casey believed that workers must learn to accept the less-than-perfect circumstances of child welfare work. (Hegar and Hunzeker (1988) asserted that public child welfare agencies are disempowering places for both workers and clients). None of the workers were optimistic about changing the current construction of child welfare practice. Casey's only suggestion was to continue to do it as it was then being done, or leave: 'You just have to come to some kind of agreement with yourself. Some people can't and they don't last very long. They need to get into an area of social work or do therapy or have a limited number of clients. It's just the nature of the beast that you have to realise that' (Casey, 22 November 1991). There was general cynicism about the possibility of smaller caseloads arising from the class action suits brought against DCFS during the 1980s even though the reform had mandated 'The maximum caseload for follow-up workers will be no more than 20 intact family cases or no more than 25 cases of children in foster care' (Illinois Department of Children and Family Services, 1992, p. 10).

Accepting current practice, however normal it may seem – 'it's so well known that the caseloads are so high that its almost silly to keep saying it over and over again' (Accardo, 30 June 1992) – had negatively affected the eight workers in this study. Workers told me of negative physical reactions which they attributed to the stress of their work. This literal embodiment of the oppressive nature of their work (Foucault, 1980; Street, 1992) 'impinges on the human's capacity for acting rationally and autonomously' (Street, 1992, p. 106). Their bodies were wearing out because of the way they had to do their work. Janine Cooper, who told me she would be in a walking frame when she was 50 because she'd be so tired, admitted, 'I have time to be a mother; I don't have time to be me. Only from nine to ten o'clock at night. It comes so late' (Cooper, 12 May 1992).

Workers reacted physically to their work by becoming depressed, sick, nauseated, and having nightmares. All the workers I spoke to admitted to some physical reaction that they blamed on either the nature of their work or on the stress produced by the amount of work. The most common physical signs told to me were dreams and nightmares. Jane Accardo made an explicit connection between her high caseload and her nightmares: 'Some nightmares, yes. Usually when my caseload gets higher, I think about it at night. When I have 35 cases I was able to leave the office and put it behind me' (Accardo, 30 June 1992). Other workers had more extreme reactions.

> (Ulcers, nightmares, sleepless nights) are part of the job. I still remember the first time I woke up and threw up. I mean, I had thrown up at other times of the day, but I'd never woken up and thrown up from anxiety. Now, unfortunately, it's a routine kind of occurrence. It should never happen (Heenan, 2 June 1992).

The most dramatic evidence of stress was one worker, not part of this study, who periodically vomited noisily into the trash basket in his office. Taina Aponte told me he had an ulcer and that he became sick when he was stressed. Her explanation was that he was the only long-serving worker on his team and so he received all the hard cases (Field notes, 14 May 1992).

Heenan mentioned to me that one female colleague had died of a heart attack at work and that another DCFS worker had shot her supervisor a few years before. (However, the worker who shot her supervisor apparently believed she was the victim of a conspiracy to fire her because of a love affair (Kass, 1988); it is not clear that the stress was work-related). Richards (1992), in his autobiographical account of child welfare work, told a similar story of a worker dying on the job and the death attributed to stress. At the same time, other researchers have found that child welfare workers themselves reported a high level of overall job satisfaction (Jayaratne and Chess, 1984). The realisation of high levels of stress and overall job satisfaction are not incompatible concepts. Job satisfaction, despite high levels of stress, may reflect workers' personal focus on the goodness and purpose of their work rather than their actual working conditions.

During the period of this research, little appeared to be done to deal with the stressful working conditions at City Office. Workers could not afford financially to take time off work: 'I could just harangue my doctor and he'd write a letter but I couldn't afford it' (Heenan, 2 June 1992). Erica Kane's supervisor showed a film on stress management at a team meeting. Erica thought he did it because 'I'm sure everybody's stressed out but I think we've been showing it more lately, more than usual, more than we have been in the past. We've been just really snappy and very frustrated and he's seen that' (Kane, 1 July 1992). Her response to increased work stress, like Casey's mentioned earlier, was to continue to accept demoralising conditions: 'there's not a whole lot you can change so it's just how you are going to deal with it differently so that it doesn't weigh on you as much.' Any effort to cope with oppressive working conditions was portrayed in individual terms. 'Make sure you take good care of yourself or you will burn out, because this will directly eat your heart out if you don't maintain a sense of humour and have some kind of philosophical perspective that will shield you somewhat from this. Do not take it personally. But it is always hard. No one can do it 100%' (Heenan, 2 July 1992). The consequence of these working conditions was that most workers did not plan long-term service in the field and workers with more experience were more dissatisfied with their jobs than workers with less experience (Fryer et al., 1988).

Interestingly, a similar situation of stressful working conditions seemed to apply also in private agencies in Chicago. Experienced workers like Janine Cooper and David Casey saw as much, and sometimes more, worker turnover in private child welfare agencies as in DCFS. While visiting with Janine Cooper, for example, a foster mother told us that the private agency workers 'change about every two months.' The foster mother found it very frustrating. She presumed that these 'young women just out of college' were changing because the pay was so low (Field notes, 9 June 1992). Bob

Heenan believed that the ongoing privatisation of child welfare services in Illinois would lead to the same pressures of overwork in private agencies as it did in DCFS. 'Once they start getting all these cases, they're going to make mistakes and they're going to get in the paper' (Heenan, 2 June 1992). The problem of worker turnover, therefore, plagued both public and private sections of child welfare practice in Cook County.

Worker solidarity

The workers in this study, while accepting the inevitability of their workloads, did act to address the immediacy of their working conditions. One of my enduring impressions of City Office was the way workers cared for other workers. I asked David Casey about the feeling of solidarity I had noticed. He agreed that there was such a feeling, fostered by the experience of common problems. 'We sometimes have a siege mentality, we feel that everybody is out to get us and its nice for you to realise that it's not just you, its the other people' (Casey, 22 November 1991). During another interview, he elaborated on the theme. For Casey, competence, permanence, direction, and mutual support are the essentials of a good team.

> If you're fortunate enough to be in a good unit where the people are competent and there isn't a whole lot of turnover, it makes everything better. You have to have a good supervisor to start things out at the top, and after that, the people have to be willing to help each other out and be able to keep an even keel sometimes when all the pressure's on. Some people can't do it (Casey, 12 May 1992).

His explanation rested within an idealised notion of the hierarchical command structure of DCFS. In fact, workers approached experienced workers like him for advice and direction, rather than their supervisors (Accardo, 20 March 1992). There was a lot of informal support and information sharing that occurred as workers sat at their desks. 'What you learn is mostly from other workers. These sessions where we sit around and talk about cases, they do two things, they let off steam, they vent a little bit and the other thing is you learn a tremendous lot about how to handle things. That's how we learn to work our way through court without getting in trouble, listening to other workers talk about it' (Reid, 1 July 1992).

Workers tended to seek advice, or 'let off steam,' with workers who were working nearby, who were physically near them. 'I've noticed nobody goes outside their teams very much. Nobody has time to answer your questions from other teams, really. So you stick pretty much with what you have on the team' (Accardo, 19 May 1992). 'Workers know each other's difficult cases. (It seems) they have spoken about it or complained about it before.

Usually, it's just letting off steam, or getting sympathy, rather than asking for help' (Field notes, 14 May 1992).

Workers were quite uninhibited in speaking out about difficulties they were having with cases. This was partly due to the lack of privacy they had when speaking on the telephone; fellow workers were often only feet away. But it was also due to the feeling of solidarity and support they received from other workers: 'I think most of the support that workers get is from their co-workers' (Valdez, 22 June 1992). Workers shared information about difficult situations with their colleagues, often telling stories against themselves or relating humorous outcomes. They sympathised with and advised colleagues who had troubles with particular judges, attorneys, and agencies. They made sure their colleagues were prepared for difficult situations: 'Over in court we go to a number of different courtrooms with different judges and different attorneys and there is a lot of change there and its good to know what the expectations of the court personnel are, because its different, and you don't want to walk in there totally cold and get surprised by some things' (Casey, 22 November 1991).

Central to worker solidarity was the initiation of new workers into their job. Ideally, more experienced workers created an atmosphere that allowed the less experienced to approach them.

> When I came to City Office, I would definitely say David Casey was very informative. In the first place that I started, there really wasn't anybody to ask anything. I think everybody was new and the supervisor was half crazy, so it was real hard to get some information. Here, you know, there's a couple of people on this team that are really knowledgeable and have been around a while; they know resources and they can give you the answer without any hassle (Accardo, 19 May 1992).

Juan Valdez learned his job the same way. Besides reading departmental policy and checking everything with his supervisor – 'I was constantly in her office the first month' – he questioned his colleagues.

> A lot of the learning I did was just talking with the other workers on my team. I drew from their experiences. I usually phrase my question, 'What would you do? If you were in this situation what would you do'? And they would tell me, 'Well, if it was me, I would do this' and I would compare what they were telling me with what my feeling was as to what would need to happen (Valdez, 14 May 1992).

Not all workers were as fortunate as Accardo and Valdez; collegial team support was not automatic. As David Casey remarked, 'Hopefully, you get on a team where people are going to help you learn' (Casey, 22 November 1991). Apparently, there were teams where new workers were not supported. Erica Kane had a supportive supervisor who eased her gradually into her work but she knew 'a lot of people who have come here, either trainees or just Child Welfare Specialist 1 (the beginning grade), and they just get cases dumped on them and they don't know what they are doing' (Kane, 20 March 1992). Yet, in this study, the workers I observed and interviewed freely gave and received advice and emotional support from their colleagues.

In addition to emotional support and sharing knowledge and advice, group solidarity also meant not further burdening colleagues by creating more work for them. When one worker on their team resigned abruptly instead of giving two weeks notice, fellow workers were critical of her because she did not take time to bring her cases up to date. This meant that other workers received cases that were incompletely documented. This resentment lingered. Four weeks after the worker abruptly resigned, I attended an Administrative Case Review with Bob Heenan. Heenan was unsure of the details of the case, mentioning that he had only received the case the week before. The Reviewer turned to me and said, 'This is what happens when someone leaves suddenly' (Field notes, 3 June 1992). There was little doubt that the worker's sudden departure had caused more work and uncertainty for her colleagues. 'In contrast, Janine Cooper said of Fran, who is on a two week honeymoon, that she'd cleared up all her cases before she left and that there had been no emergencies since she'd gone' (Field notes, 7 May 1992).

Workers could create more work for colleagues by being incompetent. Sub-groups within teams seemed to coalesce where three or four workers respected and valued each other's competence and hard work. There was little time for those who were considered incompetent. They tended to live at the edges of the group, possibly because they were seen to create work for other workers. 'There is a lot of incompetence here and it's accepted. The incompetents are shifted from one place to another and nothing is ever done, and it demoralises the ones that work hard. And in fact, the worse you are, the less work you get, and the better you are, the more work you get, to the point where it will kill you if you'll do it' (Heenan, 2 June 1992).

Incompetent people created extra work and worry for workers, thereby threatening the care and solidarity of the team and there was also the stress placed on some, more competent workers by the greater numbers and difficulty of cases they must service. Janine Cooper felt the burden, and the professional danger, of receiving cases from incompetent workers. But she placed the situation within a wider context, the sheer burden of work in some sections of DCFS: 'It's very scary when you get (a case) from another office, from certain teams specifically. A lot of that has to do with the area that they serve, they go through a lot of changes in workers' (Cooper, 12 May 1992).

Group solidarity was important to the working lives of the workers and the supervisors of the three teams I was familiar with were, I was told, supportive of their workers. It is these three teams on which I am basing my discussion. I was also told there were other teams in City Office where supervisors were not supportive. However, support for workers was localised in that the support the workers experienced came from the few fellow workers near them and their team supervisors, not from the organisation as a whole. In that sense, the impression I gained of DCFS as a whole was of an organisation that was fractured and atomised. There was not the solidarity in the total organisation that there was in the team or the group. Speaking of DCFS, the organisation, Jane Accardo put it this way, 'I don't feel real connected . . . I guess it's just so huge' (Accardo, 30 June 1992).

Media and political attacks on DCFS further distanced workers from the department. Bob Heenan told me the department was in a shambles, likening it to a rudderless ship (Field notes, 29 March 1992). He was especially critical of DCFS administrators, calling them 'cowards' when they had not supported workers attacked by judges in court (Heenan, 2 July 1992). Workers expected blame, not support, from their department: 'Most workers feel that the administration is going to punish the worker even if the worker may not have foreseen what may have gone wrong' (Valdez, 22 June 1992).

Of course, workers often criticise their organisations and so it was at DCFS. Juan Valdez noted that 'the workers are always fighting the administration. They will complain and they'll complain and they'll complain' (Valdez, 14 May 1992). Workers in this study had a litany of complaints against their department. In one sense, it did not matter whether these complaints were true or not. What they pointed to was the estrangement of the workers I studied from the department. And, while the feelings of antagonism towards administration helped reinforce small group solidarity in the teams, complaints and criticisms accentuated the alienation of the workers from the department as a whole and reinforced their feelings of embattlement and insecurity.

The following complaints underscored workers' alienation. First, workers felt isolated from the whole department. Listen to these workers: 'Everything runs really from [Head Office in another city] which has no idea what we're doing' (Heenan, 2 June 1992); 'all those people are just faceless names, even if you are trying to find one person it may take forever just to contact them' (Valdez, 22 June 1992); 'these people are seen as almost an enemy' (Reid, 1 July 1992); 'there's obviously more physical distance (and) I think more of an emotional kind of distance. We don't really know them, we don't interact with them on a daily basis, it's not as much of a comfortable feeling with them' (Kane, 1 July 1992).

Second, there was a perception among some of the more experienced workers I interviewed that the reorganisation of DCFS then underway would not reform a worsening system but was just 'shuffling things around.' 'This is just the way DCFS thinks, they reorganise every few years. They centralise and then they decentralise. They are just going to shuffle things around' (Cooper, 27 March 1992). Third, the solution proposed by the department to the fact that more cases were entering the system was to expedite cases, rather than address the causes. Workers found this stressful and distressing as it challenged their understanding of professional practice; they felt they were becoming mere bureaucrats, shuffling paperwork. Fourth, workers were powerless to change or improve the situation in which they worked: 'If something's wrong, you can't go to a person higher than you and say look, it would make more sense to do it this way, it would be better for everybody, even the agency. You just have to wait until everything is changed at once' (Heenan, 2 June 1992).

Finally, the small group solidarity within teams can be further contrasted with the seeming antagonism between different sections of the department. While team members tended to work to help each other, other sections were seen as obstructive or uncaring. Negative opinions of staff in other sections could range from Arthur Reid's comment that you have to kiss the butts of finance clerks to get what you want for kids (Field notes, 27 March 1992) to Reid's and Heenan's complaints about the staff that run the DCFS shelter. They accused shelter workers of continually obstructing and ignoring field staff. They complained that '(Shelter workers) refuse to answer phones and they leave workers waiting for hours. Both complained that the shelter seems to change the rules about every two months. That way you never know what you have to do and it gives the shelter staff more reason to send you away' (Field notes, 29 July 1991). Arlinda Delval was equally critical, 'I just was calling the shelter and you have to go to ten different people to just say three words' (Delval, 1 July 1992). All these comments spoke to a malaise in the department. Since these workers were eloquently articulate in defining this malaise, what did they do about it?

Worker resistance

At one stage in my research I wrote in my note book that workers resist the demands placed on them by doing one of three things: 'resign, transfer, or bitch about it' (Field notes, 14 May 1992). Despite the shared dissatisfaction with working conditions and the department's response or lack of it, most resistance by workers was undertaken by individuals acting alone and unnoticed. There were only few occasions where workers told me of instances when they acted to resist the social construction of their work as bureaucratic task-doing.

> In my situation, I pretty much do things on what I think would be good for people, not on what's supposed to be done. For instance, I'll visit people when they need to be, when I need to see something and want to find out something. (But) you're supposed to visit every client once a month. That's totally impossible, you couldn't do it. But if something happens they could still hold it to you. There's just certain rules that I know no one will ever monitor so as long as they don't hurt anybody, I don't follow them. I don't stick my neck out for anything risky where there could be repercussions, but there's a lot of things that are against the rules, there are no repercussions for, so I just ignore them (Heenan, 2 June 1992).

Another instance of individual resistance was Janine Cooper's keeping of certain cases when she should have transferred them. Similarly, Juan Valdez told his clients: 'If I think department policy is wrong, I'm going to tell the clients because I'm not entrenched in the system yet and I think that the clients are able to see that, that I'm a fresh face; I am someone that's not going to pull policy on them' (Valdez, 14 May 1992).

But there was little resistance beyond these individual acts. David Casey did tell me that some African-American workers would rather keep African-American children in a residential group home than have them fostered with a White family. This was to guard against African American children being fostered outside their racial group (Casey, 26 March 1991). However, the only group act of resistance I observed was instigated by Jane Accardo. She was urging Arthur Reid and Bob Heenan to take and sign a form absolving themselves of blame if anything happened to them because of their excessive caseloads. The form was addressed to their supervisor. It noted the number of cases a worker had and asked which of the cases the supervisor wanted them to service. The purpose was to draw attention to the number of cases and how difficult it was to service so many cases properly.

> We had a union meeting and so they said, basically, to cover yourself you better fill this form out so if anything should happen it'll show you have too high a caseload. Basically, the form states for our supervisors to prioritise what cases they want us to be working on, because obviously with anything over 50 (cases), it would be difficult to decide what's most important and what's not. So over here (at City Office) it's been floating around and we pretty much decided that, as our team was dwindling and we're getting higher caseloads, that we better fill this out also. I don't know if its really going to protect

you but at least it shows that you're trying (Accardo, 30 June 1992).

Even in group action, resistance was reduced to actions that would protect the individual worker rather than work toward change. Perhaps an explanation for the emphasis on the individual was the professional ideology that values the autonomy of the worker over collective action. 'Social workers like to think of themselves as independent and everybody has their own particular viewpoint that doesn't mesh with a lot of the others, so its hard to get a consensus on any of these things' (Heenan, 2 June 1992). The lack of group action in response to the oppressive nature of their work tended to call into question the meaning of the group solidarity displayed in their work. At the same time, Bob Heenan believed that initiative, whether individual or collective, was neither encouraged nor tolerated. 'Part of the thing I hate the most about the administration is how you get ahead by being very bland and not giving trouble. Any person that is critical and any person that raises questions about why things are so preposterous has no chance around here' (Heenan, 2 July 1992).

The workers' union did not appear to be a force for change. According to Heenan, 'The particular people that have the power in this union are not too great, so nothing much has happened' (Heenan, 2 June 1992). In this, the union mirrored the ennui of the workers. The union was more of a watchdog to monitor promotions and to protect workers in disfavour than an organisation working for overall change (Reid, 1 July 1992).

Staying on

How does one reconcile workers' understanding of the importance of their work, the hardships involved and their complaints about administration? Similar contradictory responses to working in child welfare have been articulated in an ethnographic study of workers in England. Corby (1987) reported on a large metropolitan social services agency in 'North City.' While some workers accepted their work without comment, and others were positive about the support it provided, many were negatively critical of their work place. They, too, were in situations where they lacked control over their work and were themselves treated as commodities, Marx's definition of alienation (Goroff, 1978). Yet, realising all of this, rather than leave DCFS, the eight workers in this study shared similar reasons for staying in public child welfare to graduate social workers in a study in northern California. The reasons given in that study included a preference for child welfare, decent wages and benefits, not being tied to a desk, and job security (Samantrai, 1992).

At City Office, a number of workers spoke about their reasons for continuing to work at DCFS. Part of the reason, for workers with some years of experience, was hesitancy at leaving DCFS to start at the bottom in some other organisation. Allied with this were the wages and medical benefits at DCFS which were considered superior to those of private child welfare agencies: financial and job security are important to workers (Fryer et al., 1989). Janine Cooper summed up this attitude thus.

> I don't want to say I do it for the money because there's not a lot of money and I have to say it, I've thought about leaving. But at my level of education, there's really nowhere for me to go right now without taking a serious pay cut. I have to be honest, that's a big part (Cooper, 12 May 1992).

While these reasons may have made working at DCFS more bearable, workers were motivated to stay by the same reasons they began working in DCFS, the protection of children. Thus, despite her working conditions, Erica Kane was still committed, 'I like the general idea of what I'm doing' (Kane, 20 March 1992). So, too, was Jane Accardo although she rejected the impossible burden placed on her that her job was to produce perfect families.

> I think they (media) want these perfect families to be sitting there when you're done with the case; that these parents will never abuse their kids, will never drink, will never use drugs, will supervise their kids totally appropriately, will never date somebody who might kill their children, things like that. We can only just deal with a couple of their problems. (Accardo, 19 May 1992).

Arthur Reid cautiously agreed, typically understating his reasons for staying: 'I think most of the time the best we can do is to do a little bit more good than harm, that's all' (Reid, 23 March 1992). It was the idealism of what they want to do, the ideals of child protecting and child saving, that kept workers at their work when they had so few successes and so many setbacks. Their reasons for staying in DCFS, then, originated in the same child protecting stories that explained why they started in DCFS.

This chapter articulated the varieties of stress in child welfare practice and showed how those stresses impact on the lives of the workers and of their clients. Particular attention was paid to the stresses that come from child welfare practice itself as well as stresses that come from the way the workers must carry out that practice. I have noted the ways in which they band together to confront the burden of what they do. Finally, workers stay in child welfare work for the same reason they started in that work, their belief that protecting children is important. In the next chapter, I will reflect on the working lives of the eight people I studied and the implications for child welfare practice.

8 Redoing child welfare practice

This project explored the working lives of eight child welfare workers. In their own words, and through my interpretation of their practice, they answered the question, 'How do child welfare workers understand and live the experience of doing child welfare work?' In detail, they outlined their views of themselves and their work, their understandings of their clients, both children and adults, and the negative and positive meanings child welfare work has for workers. Working lives that were overburdened, stressful and sometimes dangerous provided bleak explanations of child welfare work. Yet their often pessimistic views were complemented by the importance and worth they saw in their profession, the protection of children. This chapter looks again at their work and proposes a critical reframing of child welfare practice.

Working in child welfare

The study found that the current practice of child welfare harms clients as much as it helps them. This harm comes about despite the work, sincerity, and dedication of child welfare workers and the (voluntary and involuntary) cooperation of the children and families who are child welfare's clients. It comes about because the ideology of child-saving coupled with the homogenising use of bureaucratic routinisation and the huge numbers of cases erases the personal in its quest for total efficiency. In studying the lived experience of child welfare workers at City Office I found that current practice has become demeaning and disempowering for workers and clients alike. There are three themes that sum up my understanding of child welfare work as I experienced it in this research. The themes are protection, relationships, and stress. I will consider these themes and comment on the invisibility of Native American families and children in the child welfare practice of City Office.

Protecting children was a central theme in the workers' biographies. They believed that there were children who needed state intervention to protect them. In this belief, the workers placed themselves within national and international social work and humanitarian efforts to better children's lives. Through their belief in their mission to protect children they grounded themselves in a history of child protection that goes back over a hundred years. Workers' beliefs about their work answered my question about how they understood their practice. However, when I set out to understand how they lived out their protecting of children in their day-to-day work, I saw that the demands and conditions of their work thwarted their child protection ideals. The disjuncture between their ideals and the reality of their work caused them stress and disillusionment. Their day-to-day experience accentuated the tension in child welfare practice between the theory and the reality of practice.

My interpretation of the lived experience of child welfare workers at City Office should not be taken as a criticism of child protection itself. Child protection is still a necessary field of practice. There are still many children who are abused and neglected and need state intervention and removal from abusive situations. But the child removal and foster care system is imploding under the sheer number of children coming into care. The cause of those numbers is the pattern of reaction by investigators to remove children (Sarri and Finn, 1992) and the long, involved process needed to return them home.

From my conversations with workers and my reading of case files, I found, and workers confirmed, that there are children who may have been indicated as abused or neglected but they should not be receiving child protective services at all. Speaking of one family on her caseload, Janine Cooper was adamant that the only type of services she could provide and monitor – services aimed at rectifying maltreatment – were unsuitable for her clients.

> Even though these parents aren't following this Order and something else clearly needs to be done, I don't feel that the parents are going to hurt their children, they're not abusive people. They're just guilty of very bad judgment but the judge isn't going to see it that way (Cooper, 12 May 1992).

Juan Valdez felt the same way about many of the parents he worked with. These parents were not malicious or abusive; they needed services different from those that presumed they were.

100

That is something I struggle with all the time. Every parent makes mistakes and unless it's a situation where the children were truly at risk of dying, I think that what the parents need is support to make sure they don't make the mistakes. But I don't feel it's necessary to remove the children the first time they mess up (Valdez, 14 May 1992).

Removing children from parents who were 'guilty of bad judgment' or who had made 'mistakes' subverted the child protection system, used up scarce foster parent resources, and created burdens of anguish and guilt for children and parents.

Bob Heenan also spoke to the same misidentification of children as abused or neglected when he asserted that the focus of child protection was awry. Child welfare practice merely documented individual failure rather than addressed the causes of abuse and neglect.

I think after working with thousands and thousands of people, it's become more clear that they set this system up before they realised what it was supposed to do. And a lot of things that we're doing here are just measuring effects where our social system fails, and all we're doing is just documenting the failures. And we don't ever change the causes so that they don't continue. (If), you know, education, health care, personal safety, people, values, everything doesn't change then none of this abuse and neglect can change. You can't work it backwards, person-by-person, and change society. I think that's what they thought they could do, that you could just remedy these few bad apples then we'd have all good parents. But if you have everybody living in a society that doesn't value children and that is as stressful and hard on people as ours is, you're going to have these problems (Heenan, 2 June 1992).

When it is predominantly minority and poor children in Illinois who are receiving 'protection' from abuse and neglect (Massat, 1992), Heenan's broadening definition of child welfare practice further situated individual acts of abuse and neglect within the then US national policy discourse on education, health care, and personal safety. This discourse placed child welfare, in its broad sense as the general welfare of children, on the political agendas of inner-city neighbourhoods and national debates. It prompts a redefinition of the current simplistic framing of child welfare problems as only abuse and neglect (Pelton, 1991).

Officially, in DCFS brochures and child welfare textbooks, child welfare work has been portrayed as sensitive, relational, and creative. In reality, court-ordered and DCFS-approved practice emphasised bureaucratic inflexibility and work that did not require initiative or relationship skills. Yet workers attempted to resist that definition and much of what they did revolved around their ability to create and sustain a series of relationships with clients, court personnel, and fellow practitioners. For example, workers learned and used negotiating skills with all sections of their working world, clients, court staff, private agency staff, and administrators and other staff in DCFS. Without these negotiating abilities, workers were unable to do their job. This disjuncture in perception between the skilled nature of what they did and the official perception of them as mere clerks was a source of annoyance and resentment among workers and reinforced Germain and Gitterman's (1980) contention that work contexts can create barriers to the helping process.

In contrast to the bureaucratic configuring of their work, the workers in this study valued the opportunity to gain more time to establish relationships with their clients. Protecting children, therefore, was not just providing services or direction but building and maintaining a professional partnership with clients. Admittedly, some workers such as Jane Accardo did not want clients to become 'buddies,' professional and hierarchical distance were maintained. Even so, workers spoke positively and excitedly of instances when they had the time to build relationships with clients. Janine Cooper, of course, negotiated with her supervisor to ensure that she held on to cases for many years in order to maintain such a relationship. The importance of building relationships between workers and clients was more than just to ensure that they could get along together; relationships are the basis of social work practice. Workers spoke to me with regret that they could not spend more time with all their clients and build relationships with them similar to the ones they had with those clients who had triumphed over their problems.

Nowhere was the disjuncture in worker-client relationships between the ideal and the real more apparent than in the homogenisation of all clients into a generic client that all services and all responses had to fit. Irrespective of the class, gender, or racial backgrounds of clients the same services were provided to all. The homogenisation of clients into 'the client' cut clear across the individual differentiation required in a helping relationship. Performing bureaucratic work which did not require forming helping relationships with clients reinforced the hierarchical, distancing stance of workers towards clients and continued the domination of both. When the way their work was organised prevented them from having a relationship with their clients, workers felt cheated and devalued. As became clear in this project, the bureaucratic erasure of the individual self of the client also erased the individual self of the worker.

The value and utility of workers' partnerships with colleagues are important findings of this study. As they valued professional relationships with clients, so too did workers value their relationships with their colleagues. Within their shared understanding of the purpose of child protection, workers looked to nearby colleagues to support and guide their work. These small groups appeared to be havens from the stresses of work where colleagues could unwind from the demands of the job and ask for guidance in managing their cases. It was also clear from this study that collegial relationships tended to operate only at a team or intra-team level; workers did not experience the same feeling of collegiality outside their small working groups.

Within the bureaucratic nondifferentiation of child welfare practice at City Office, Indian children were virtually lost among the caseloads. For a start, only a few workers had Indian cases and only a few cases on a caseload were Indian. This ensured that Indian cases were seen as just one or two among many cases of abuse or neglect. Second, the main concern of workers and attorneys was bureaucratic, to make sure that the more stringent legal provisions in regard to Indian children were observed. A typical attitude was this from a lawyer at Juvenile Court, defining the minimal level of involvement needed: 'Oh, it is an Indian case. We have to prove beyond a reasonable doubt' (Field notes, 22 June 1992). While this approach fulfilled one of the legal requirements of ICWA it in no way meant that Indian children had a specific kind of child welfare practice designed for them 'to prevent the breakup of Indian families' as ICWA requires. Indian children were treated just like the rest of the children that came into care. The subsuming of Indian children under the notion of the generic client underlined their invisibility in City Office.

By focusing on workers with Indian clients I was able to make Native American children and families more visible. But, this visibility only reinforced the finding that they, too, are administered in such a way that their distinctiveness does not become a basis for differentiated services. When Native American children and families were given the same undifferentiated services as all the other clients of City Office, these services were a continuation of assimilatory practices that have formed racist attitudes and policies over the last hundred years. Furthermore, child welfare practice at City Office and in Juvenile Court, in so far as they continued the homogenisation of all clients into one generic client, contravened the Federal Government's commitment to Indian self-determination (National Indian Policy Center, 1992). The wider policy context of Indian self-determination appeared to have no place in child welfare practice at City Office.

The stress placed on workers was one of my enduring memories of this research. It was not just the stress of having to work with abused and neglected children. That was to be expected and is unavoidable. But the way public child welfare work at City Office was organised – high case loads, excessive paperwork, personal danger, unsympathetic courts – produced extra pressures that tarnished and frustrated the work. City

Office's situation was not atypical. Workers told me of other area offices in Cook County DCFS where work pressures were worse than theirs (Field note, 1 July 1992: 'Arthur Reid just told me that he talked to someone from another Area Office and she has 147 cases, 107 kids and 40 families'). Nor was the situation in Illinois DCFS atypical. In fact, commentators have noted that crises similar to City Office's are typical of child welfare services throughout the United States (Hartman, 1990; Pecora et al., 1989; Pelton, 1990). This research is a singular instance of a universal trend and that is its importance.

Issues of child protection, relationships among workers and between workers and clients, and job-related stress have implications for practice. But if the response to this study is merely to change, tighten up, and modify current practice then the result will be just more of the same. This study has shown that the current way of doing child welfare is inherently counterproductive for workers and clients. As we draw near to what I suspect future commentators will see as the beginning of the end of the second child-saving phase of child protection, the need is to reverse current practice not reshape and reform it.

Implications for practice

Any application of this research to practice must center around the misfocus of child protective services, the bureaucratisation of workers' relationships with clients, and the creation of work contexts that value the development of helping relationships between workers and clients. I will briefly highlight each of these issues in a challenge to current practice.

Somehow, over the last 30 years, child welfare has become dominated by child protective services (Kamerman and Kahn, 1990; Sarri and Finn, 1992). The highjacking of child welfare into a reactive, punitive service and the subsequent application of technical skills to passive, acquiescent (female) clients has resulted in practice that is narrowly focused, biased against women, racist, and counterproductive. For both clients and workers, the continuation of practice as it is currently administered is to continue up a deadend where the burgeoning crisis in child welfare services will only become worse.

Pelton (1991) was right when he asserted that the framing of child welfare problems in terms of abuse and neglect was too simplistic. The realisation that it is poor and minority families who, in the main, form the pool from which the foster care population is drawn (Pelton, 1990) should reinforce the perception that the primary emphasis in child welfare practice should be on prevention. Back in 1983, a report for the Illinois state legislature about Illinois DCFS recommended as much in the following words:

As our investigation progressed, we began to realise that the current focus of efforts directed toward the problem of child abuse and neglect must change drastically at some point. Efforts expended on treating abuse and neglect after the fact are not only a poor use of public funds, but also ultimately self-defeating. Primary prevention must be given the same priority as treatment (Illinois Legislative Investigating Commission, 1983, p. ix).

A preventive focus for child welfare will begin with political efforts to ensure that available monies for child welfare services will be reallocated to favour preventive services over substitute care. The extent to which child protection drives child welfare services in the United States can be gauged from the fact that 84% of federal funding for child welfare services in fiscal year 1990 was directed to substitute care and adoption assistance (Pelton, 1990). If the ratio could be reversed and the same proportion of money spent on prevention as is currently spent on substitute care and adoption assistance, what City Office child welfare workers see as the punishing and traumatising of many children taken into foster care would be mitigated. In addition, children would be assisted within their families, thereby fulfilling the family preservation provisions of the Adoption Assistance and Child Welfare Act of 1980. Furthermore, if only children suffering severe cases of child abuse and neglect were removed from their families, or if removal was seen only as a last resort rather than a first option, the numbers of children in substitute care would drop even more significantly. In such a scenario, the foster care system would no longer be overburdened and workers' regrets that they can't find suitable foster parents for their child clients would not be applicable.

Pelton (1990) has suggested that the term 'child harm' is a better description of what happens to most children deemed abused and neglected than child abuse. The realisation that 'child abuse and neglect' are strongly related to poverty and minority status argues for a multicausal understanding of child harm in place of current simplistic assumptions of parental abuse. Hutchison (1990) contends that the conventional formulation of child abuse in terms of incidence, cause, treatment, and prevention does not address the way in which child abuse and neglect cases come to public attention. Nor does the conventional formulation tell what motivates action by public authorities (Gelles, 1983). The interactionist approach considers child maltreatment from the combined perspectives of child, adult, and environment (Hutchison, 1990). From this perspective, environmental and social factors interact with personal and psychological factors to contribute to individual abuse. Individual pathology, racial and

105

cultural bias, social deviance, and poverty are all elements in the social construction of a particular child as abused or neglected. An interactionist perspective which values multiple causation for definition and response to child maltreatment recognises that total agreement on what is abuse is unlikely (Gelles, 1983). This perspective is congruent with the daily problematic reality of child welfare work. With its similarity to ecological theories of social work and to the life model of practice (Germain and Gitterman, 1980), an interactionist perspective contributes an holistic setting for child welfare practice that considers the child in the differing interactive contexts that are its environment. This approach also values community and systems responses because of the multilayered social and physical conditions that lead to abuse and neglect. A preventive stance implies coordination with mental health, general health, and educational services (Sundel and Homan, 1979). It also implies coordination with community groups such as churches, unions, neighbourhood groups and with police, judges, and attorneys.

Such an interactionist, multicausal understanding of intervention is at odds with the current case-management approach. Case-management is easily subverted to a regulation-driven understanding of service provision that does not take into account the nuances of individual difference. Case-management that focuses only on a checklist of services based on psychological explanations for abuse and neglect cannot address the causes of child-harm nor provide services to alleviate the conditions that create harm for children.

Finally, the assumption underlying current child welfare practice that all cases are the same reinforces the inappropriate use of 'the majority of the intervention theories and models cited in the literature (which) have focused on the white family and may not be appropriate for ethnic-minority families' (Mokuau, 1990, p. 607). The current child welfare system is a 'white' system, drawing its values, beliefs, and interventions from what white, middle-class Americans consider good for children. Janine Cooper's and Jane Accardo's biographies speak eloquently about this interpretation of child protection. Within a non-homogeneous, multiracial, multicultural society, 'white' child welfare seeks to assimilate and devalue non-white families and cultural values. An appropriate reinterpretation of child protection will support the dismantling of the current monolith of child protection in favour of locally- and ethnically-controlled child welfare services. For Native Americans, for example, the intent of ICWA is better served if the case management of Native American children in public agency care is transferred to Native American child welfare agencies (McMahon and Gullerud, 1995).

Reinventing relationships

Reinterpreting child protection in the way I have outlined above necessitates placing value on developing relationships with clients. A change in policy and practice to keep most children with their mothers and not to remove them would allow workers to work preventively with families, the opposite of their current attempts to return children to dislocated families. This would require a less antagonistic and less legalistic stance by workers toward clients. It would require a more dialogical relationship (Freire, 1970, 1985) with clients where expert worker knowledge and local client knowledge are both valued as part of protecting children. Weick (1992) urges the reactivation in social work of Foucault's (1980) call for the recognition of people's own experience. Child welfare practice that values cooperative learning and cooperative intervention, where workers and clients act together to address occasions of child harm, values both clients' experience and workers' expertise. In such a dialogical relationship neither workers nor clients are silenced. This cooperation would mirror the valued, but infrequent, times the City Office workers were able to work in partnership with their clients.

Such a change demands a new understanding of parents (mothers) and children in the management of a case. They can no longer be treated as objects to be acted upon, learners to be taught, but they must be seen as subjects of their own lives, able to engage in cooperative participation in their own healing (Weick, 1992) and transformation (Freire, 1985). Certainly, it is apparent from this research that workers not only value the building of a relationship with a family over a period of time but they see time spent in this relationship-building as being the more likely to give a positive result in child protection terms. Case-management procedures that emphasise the technical delivery of services will not be able to service children and families to address the causes of child harm. 'Child and family services must develop richer, more effective interventions to respond to the complex and intertwined needs of children and families' (Kamerman and Kahn, 1990, p. 13).

There are also implications for social work education and training if workers' yearnings for a more dialogical relationship with their clients are to be taken seriously. Education and training that continue to emphasise the social control and domination of the poor, minorities, and women cannot continue. Purely technical applications of skills can have no place in a profession which purports to value the self-determination of the individual, the importance of shared goals and the political reconstruction of society in social justice to produce change. We need to emphasise a social work that empowers workers and clients rather than leads to the oppression and domination of both, that enables collaboration rather than mandates control, and that emphasises engagement between workers and clients rather than detachment and antagonism.

Dialogue with others is not just a speech form but work and action (Agger, 1991). 'The issue . . . is not simply the theory of emancipation; it is the practice of it as well' (Horkheimer, 1989, p. 200). Since current child welfare practice is one form of oppression for women, minorities and the poor, a challenge for social work is to continue Jane Addams' (1910/1981) project of interpreting democracy in social terms. Young (1990) has argued that contemporary theories of justice tend to be individualistic, neglecting the social contexts of citizens as members of groups that are more or less subject to social and political oppression. She puts forward an idea of social justice that refers 'not only to distribution, but also to the institutional conditions necessary for the development and exercise of individual capacities and collective communication and cooperation' (Young, 1990, p. 39). To theorise social work action in terms of social justice is consonant with the ideals of social work and of Jane Addams' original project of interpreting democracy in social terms.

In contemporary terms, interpreting democracy in social terms means challenging the political arrangements that exclude women, minorities and the poor from a socially just participation in society (Young, 1990). Young has detailed five faces of oppression – exploitation, marginalisation, powerlessness, cultural imperialism, and violence – that distort communication, give rise to social injustice, and foil political participation. These oppressions are the contexts in which individual acts of abuse and neglect occur and thrive and in which child welfare work at City Office, and elsewhere, takes place. A reconfiguration of child welfare practice means reinventing the relationships workers and clients have with each other in order to create, in work and action (Agger, 1991), a process of democratic participation. Ultimately, it means engaging the stories of child welfare workers and child welfare clients with those sections of American society that frame the social construction of child abuse. To say that clients or workers are unworthy or incapable of that is to place them outside democratic society, something we cannot do.

There is also a continuing need to explore the ways practitioners understand and experience their professional practice. This project has only touched on issues of race, class, and gender and the further exploration of these issues as contexts for child welfare practice is important. Naturally, I make a strong claim for the use of ethnographic observation and interviewing in pursuing that research, so that the voices and the lived experience of participants are heard. This project attempted a broad sweep of eight workers and, in some ways, sacrificed individual depth for common understandings shared by many workers. Future studies by researchers of a different age, race, gender, and cultural background than myself would help to create a richer, more textured understanding of child welfare practice.

I researched follow-up workers. Future ethnographic research on investigators would be especially valuable for understanding the professional judgement and the contextual norms that serve to indicate a child as abused and neglected. The work of private agency workers is vital for the assessment of mothers' fitness to have their children returned to them. Research on private agency workers would be valuable for understanding child welfare practice as would research on attorneys and judges from the Juvenile Court. Above all, research that centred and privileged clients' understandings of child welfare practice would be a particularly valuable addition to knowledge. There is scope here for considering children, mothers, fathers, and foster mothers within the different economic and racial contexts where children are indicated for abuse or neglect.

Reprise

What, then, is the meaning of this project and its interpretation of the lived experience of the workers at City Office? Fundamentally, the eight workers have given a critique of their work and their profession that cuts to the soul of what child welfare is about. They have shown in their words, their actions, and their bodies that there is a basic misdirection in current practice that needs to be addressed. They have seen that misdirection acted out on the children and families who are their clients and they know that something needs to change.

Nationally, the time has come, since the obvious failure of the reforms of the Adoption Assistance and Child Welfare Act (Hartman, 1990; Pelton, 1991), to realign the purpose of child protection. Child protection is important and there are many workers committed to the protection of children. But if child welfare services continue to harm children, families, and workers in the way I found and have described at City Office, then the nightmarish practice outlined in these pages will persist as well. Ann Weick has written 'the strengths perspective supports a vision of knowledge universally shared, creatively developed, and capable of enhancing individual and communal growth' (1992, p. 24). This perspective offers a new direction for child welfare, radically different from the fixation on pathology and human deficiency that drives current child welfare practice. Child welfare practice needs a new perspective and new alliances that will value the knowledge of workers, families, and children in a partnership for children's welfare. I have argued as much in this project.

Methodological appendix

This appendix describes the research methods I used to understand how public agency child welfare workers understand and go about their work. Within an interpretive perspective which values thinking that is reflective, historical, comparative, and biographical (Denzin, 1989a), the research question frames both the subjects whom the researcher studies and the personal history of the researcher. Framing the research question involves five steps. These are, locate in one's own personal history the biographical experience to be studied; discover how this private trouble becomes a public issue that affects many lives, institutions and social groups; locate the sites where people with these troubles do things together; begin to ask how these experiences occur; and formulate the question in a single statement (Denzin, 1989a, p. 49): 'How do child welfare workers understand and live the experience of doing child welfare work?' This appendix delineates the ethnographic methods I used to describe, classify, and interpret (Denzin, 1989b) the worlds of the child welfare workers

This research is biographical. It presents the experiences and definitions of child welfare workers as they are interpreted by the workers themselves. Their stories are histories, focussing on the process of the events that convey the lived experience (Denzin, 1989b) of child welfare workers. In Max Weber's evocative phrase – human beings as animals suspended in webs of significance they themselves have spun – I follow Geertz's definition for the analysis of culture as interpretation in search of enigmatic meaning (Geertz, 1973).

In undertaking ethnographic research I have chosen a research process that 'closely observes, records, and engages in the daily life' of child welfare workers, and then 'writes accounts of this culture, emphasising descriptive detail ' (Marcus and Fischer, 1986, p. 18). Yet ethnography is more than just recording an objective reality 'out there' (Clifford and Marcus, 1986; Denzin,

1989b). Writing ethnographically is a creative process. It is both interactive and interpretive and relies on the ethnographer to produce a qualitative narrative that conveys the ways the subjects make sense of their social worlds.

Gaining entry

Gaining entry to a research site means negotiation with multiple gatekeepers, both formal and informal (Lincoln and Guba, 1985). Many researchers, however, ignore the reporting of this most important phase of the research. Pithouse (1987) and Corby (1987), whose studies are similar, glossed over any mention of gaining entree to their research sites in their reports. Dingwall et al. (1983), in a similar study, merely stated that 'John Eekelaar developed contacts with the social services department' (p. 25). Yet, it would be realistic to expect some difficulties in gaining access to public child welfare agencies: Johnson (1975), for example, has noted the difficulty of gaining access to large bureaucratic organisations, including public agencies. The process I undertook was as follows.

Lincoln and Guba (1985, p. 251) presume that, before beginning formal research, 'the inquirer has made every effort to become thoroughly acquainted with the field sites in which the study is to take place.' In January 1991, I spoke with DCFS research and planning executives at their Head Office about my research and left them a written outline of my proposal for preliminary research. They were receptive to my presentation and at their suggestion I contacted two DCFS administrators for Cook County, Chicago. Both read my proposal and agreed to it. In March 1991, I obtained written permission from Illinois DCFS to interview child welfare workers who have Native American clients and 15 months later, after seeking further permission, I was allowed access to the case records of clients important to this research.

When I contacted the relevant administrator in Chicago about my research, he offered to call two supervisors at City Office, a DCFS office with Indian child welfare cases. One of the supervisors recommended David Casey, a worker known as knowledgeable and experienced in working with Indian clients, as the best person to begin talking to. In due course, I spoke with other workers Casey recommended and then with workers in another team whom their supervisor told me had Indian cases. I also informally interviewed workers who did not have Native American cases at the time of the research but had in the past. For these informal interviews I received individual oral permission from each worker, as ethical practice demands (Lincoln and Guba, 1985), after explaining who I was and what I was interested in.

From March, 1991 to April 1992, I made over 30 day long visits to City Office. In May and June, 1992, I lived in Chicago three days a week so as to have easier access to City Office. Over these 16 months, I interviewed workers, both informally and in structured sessions which I tape-recorded, and I accompanied them to Juvenile Court, to visit clients, and to visit other agencies. In the beginning, because I was in the process of becoming acquainted with the research site, I interviewed and accompanied workers whether they had Indian clients or not. Later, for the research, I identified eight follow-up workers who were managing Native American cases and these agreed to be part of the research. These eight workers took part in a series of three taperecorded interviews each that described their Indian cases and their daily work, their own biographies and their approach to practice. Some interview questions were based on Jansen (1992). Before tape-recording an interview I asked each person to read, agree to and sign two consent forms; one I kept and one I returned to them. I also had many short discussions with these and other workers. These discussions were written directly into my field notebook.

Securing empirical experience

The gathering of information about a person, place or process relies on detailed descriptions, direct quotations, and excerpts from documents, correspondence, records and case histories (Patton, 1980). This information is gathered by the researcher who observes people in different situations, interviews the participants, and studies documents that arise from and bear on the situations observed. The ethnographer then interprets the information in the writing up of the research.

The use of participant observation within the context of this research was guided by Denzin (1989b). He saw participant observation as combining interviewing, document analysis, direct observation, and observer participation. The combination and use of these multiple methods to study the same phenomenon is called triangulation. Adopting a triangulated perspective demonstrates sophisticated rigour in research methods by making the use of multiple methods, sources of information, and interactionally grounded interpretations as public as possible. The use of procedures involving interviewing, document analysis, direct observation, and observer participation is based on the assumption that the use of multiple methods is necessary to understand empirical reality. 'The interpretive interactionist attempts to live his or her way into the lives of those being investigated' (Denzin, 1989a, p. 42).

Participating in the social world of child welfare workers and making careful recordings in field notes of the problematic and mundane features of their work guides the researcher to understand their world as they do. Gold (1958) has discussed four possible roles for observers that range from complete detached observation to complete involvement and participation in the site. The participant observer attempts 'to render the world meaningful from the perspective of those studied' (Denzin, 1989a, p. 42) and this is usually done by participating directly in the various activities that constitute the subject's world. I participated when I accompanied workers in visits to Juvenile Court, to private agencies, to visit clients and when I took part in office discussions and meetings. At court, I listened and observed as each worker negotiated with attorneys, clients, and private agency staff. When the case was called before the judge, I attended the court hearing and continued my observations. I sat at the back of the court, although this position lessened my ability to overhear what each participant was saying, because it was not appropriate to approach closer to the bench to observe.

In the office, I was a participant in informal discussions about work, about cases, and about concerns of the workers. How much to participate is a question of professional judgment. Usually I tried to balance observation and participation, as Bogdan and Biklen (1982) recommend. Sometimes there were situational constraints that only allowed me to observe. This was so in Juvenile Court. At other times, I both participated and observed, especially when transporting children with a worker or being introduced to clients or agency staff. Then, common courtesy demanded some interaction. Once, for the safety of a small child whom a worker was taking from her home with the assistance of the police, I volunteered my help to hold the screaming child while the worker drove the car. The parents, other relatives, and neighbours were yelling abuse and one youth threw a bucket of water at the worker. Even then, though, I was observing as much as I could. Perhaps this is what Bogdan and Biklen mean when they say 'becoming a researcher means internalising the research goal while collecting data in the field' (1982, p. 129).

I structured my observations by using a simplified list of the nine dimensions of data collecting advised by Spradley (1980). These are, space (the layout of the office, client's house, other agency's office), actors (the people involved in the situations and their names), activities (the various related activities of the people in the setting), objects (the physical elements present, for example the furniture and its layout), acts (actions of individuals), events (the particular actions of individuals in a structured situation), time (the time sequence in the office, work times, breaks, lunch hours), goals (the activities people are attempting to accomplish in particular situations as well as the differences between the goals of DCFS staff, clients, and staff from other agencies), and feelings (emotions in particular contexts). While observing, I jotted down descriptions and

113

snatches of conversation. Later in the day and always before I went to bed, I wrote out an extended account of the day under each of the nine headings. Spradley's list not only structured my observations but allowed me greater facility to recall what I had observed.

Workers were, at times, reluctant to have me accompany them on visits to clients. Sometimes this was openly stated as when Janine Cooper felt that my presence would be an added pressure on a woman who was in the process of having her six children removed from her care. I respected her judgment and did not go with her. Once or twice I sensed some reluctance on the part of one or two workers to have me come with them to visit clients. Whether this was on account of their reluctance to have me observe them at work or their concern for the clients, I do not know. I, however, was fairly insistent on my wish to accompany them unless I was given an outright refusal. While aware that there are times when workers cannot take a researcher with them, my dilemma was that I did not want to meet only 'tame' clients but a cross-section of those who receive DCFS' services. When I went with workers to visit Indian clients, the workers had already asked the clients if I could accompany them. No one refused, to my knowledge. When accompanying workers who were visiting non-Indian clients, I was usually introduced as a colleague or a visitor from Australia studying child welfare.

Sometimes I went with workers to neighbourhoods that they described as dangerous. Once, in a house in one suburb, known as 'murder capital of Chicago' or so I was told, I stood apprehensively in the hallway of a house while two policemen and a worker took an African American child from her parents. I wrote in my notebook, 'Amid the crying, weeping, cursing, and screaming, I stood in the hallway, conscious of my intrusion, not wanting to go in or leave, but uncomfortably aware that I would be seen as a cause of the commotion.' Visiting the public housing project of Riverside Meadows, for example, I imitated the child welfare workers by dressing in nondescript clothes and leaving my credit cards and most of my money at the office, in case we were robbed. These were situations the workers faced every day.

Interviewing is the classic sociological research method (Denzin, 1989b). The purposes of interviewing are to explore and gather experiential material as a resource for understanding some interactional situation and to develop and probe the meaning of that experience (van Manen, 1990). The interview is a gift of time and conversation (Denzin, 1989b) shaped by the questions of the interviewer. Within an interpretive framework, an interview is constructed jointly by the interviewer and the respondent (Mishler, 1986).

Open-ended interviewing is the most appropriate form of interviewing for this type of research (Denzin, 1989a). In the beginning, I interviewed workers and other staff fairly informally. Later, I had directed conversations with the same workers to amplify and clarify knowledge that I had gained. During more extended interviews I probed respondents for more information (Lincoln and Guba, 1985) using what I had learned in one interview to clarify, probe, and question in the next.

The purpose of all of these interviews was to understand the meanings staff give to their work experiences and to triangulate my emerging understandings. Because of the developing relationship with workers many of the interviews approximated creative interviewing where two persons openly share understandings with one another in a search for greater self-understanding (Denzin, 1989a). I interviewed a broader cross-section of people than the eight workers who were the focus of my study so as to understand the organisational context of the workers. Thus, I also interviewed supervisors, Head Office staff, and other DCFS staff. In regard to Native American children, parents, and child welfare workers with whom the DCFS child welfare workers interacted, I visited and interviewed representatives from three Native American organisations in Chicago. I also interviewed two attorneys whose agencies were engaged in lawsuits against DCFS. All this helped set a context for the understanding of the day-to-day work of the DCFS child welfare workers by sharing in their work life and symbolic world (Denzin, 1989b).

Interviews with DCFS workers generally took place at their desks surrounded by the paraphernalia and demands of their work. At times, other workers joined in the interview and added their comments and opinions. The demands of clients, supervisors, and other workers all intruded and interviews had to be stopped, truncated or postponed. However, workers were gracious in giving me their time and ensuring, as much as they could, that we were not interrupted. Some sense of this comes from an entry in my fieldnotes of November 23, 1991.

> The interviews I conducted were in the workers' offices surrounded by the sounds of work, telephones, other workers coming in and out. Dave Casey took out the cord from the back of his phone so it wouldn't ring and disturb us. Suzanne Hamilton obviously had plenty to do but she still agreed to go ahead with the interview as we'd planned. However, I did offer to see her another time and, when she said it was alright to go ahead, I limited the interview to half an hour.

The demands of their work ensured that workers spent a lot of time outside the office. Toward the end of my research, after a number of workers had resigned or transferred and additional pressures were put on those that remained, the whole building appeared quieter and emptier than when I first visited City Office. Workers were also working harder and were more difficult to talk to because of their extra cases and responsibilities. Fewer workers, however, meant more office space and I was given an office with a desk that made writing and recording easier and more private.

Documents and records make up a large part of the work of child welfare workers. Public documents include official policies and mission statements, official statistics and reports, laws, media accounts, and posters. Some workers gave me or recommended reports for me to read. One downstate worker supplied me with DCFS' brochures on investigation, foster care, and adoption. Case notes, however, were not readily available. I sought and received special permission to read the case files of the Native American children I was researching. Case notes, because of their summary nature, should not be over-emphasised as a source of information. 'When you get a transfer summary, especially depending on who writes the summary, it doesn't really tell you much about what's going on and what kind of little things are going on in there that might explode at any given time' (Cooper, 12 May 1992). Pithouse (1987, p. 25) came to the conclusion that, written records, as well as other official indices, are 'more likely to obfuscate than reveal the way work is routinely accomplished.'

The production of case notes is one of the ways social work practice is made visible – they are 'the evidence of unobserved encounters' (Pithouse, 1987, p. 33). Case notes are important because they reflect the worker's orientation to the client. 'The information that is compiled about a client is almost entirely the product of the worker's communications' (Jacobs, 1970, p. 250). Case notes, therefore, as paperwork, are examples of 'the formal structures of everyday activities' (Garfinkel and Sacks, 1970/1990, p. 63) that encapsulate what child welfare work is. At City Office, workers spent at least three days a week in the office producing paperwork which was entered in clients' files.

Trustworthiness is the researcher's persuasion of the reader that the research findings are credible (Lincoln and Guba, 1985). Invalidity can originate, for example, in the 'multiple, conflicting identities, selves, and rules' (Denzin, 1989b, p. 113) that characterise the interactional tension of an interview. Cross-gender interviews, interviews that are not private but given in a public context, power differences that come from race, status, age, or any other reason, all may affect the validity of the information gained. To maintain trustworthiness, I followed a number of procedures recommended in research texts. I carried a notebook in which I wrote down conversations, observations, notes to myself, and lists of emerging themes. As well, I made myself charts of the number and types of interviews, observations, and readings of case files to make sure I covered each of the workers and their Indian clients. I maintained a reflective journal in which I noted methodological decisions, reflections on my own performance, and reflections on literature relevant to my study. I triangulated by re-interviewing workers to check my emerging hypotheses. I also attended a weekly discussion group with other researchers engaged in qualitative research where research dilemmas and problems were aired. As well, I had 'a noninvolved professional peer' (Lincoln and Guba, 1985, p. 283) with whom I could debrief. Debriefing included exploring methodological decisions and future plans, critiquing self-presentation, maintaining perspective in the research, and reading drafts of the research. Finally, I gave the workers at City Office an opportunity to read my accounts and incorporated their feedback in my interpretation.

Interpreting empirical experience

The next step was to make sense of the descriptions that had been gathered: interpretation builds on description and is the attempt to explain the meaning of a term or process (Denzin, 1989a). Interpretation is an on-going process. Yet, as a research process, ethnographic observation is deliberately unstructured so as to maximise the discovery of interpretations. Instead of beginning with set hypotheses the intent is to continually revise and refine emergent hypotheses as the research proceeds (Denzin, 1989b). 'The process of data analysis, then, is essentially a synthetic one, in which the constructions that have emerged (been shaped by) inquirer-source interactions are reconstructed into meaningful wholes' (Lincoln and Guba, 1985, p. 333). During the course of the field research I periodically made lists of ideas that occurred to me as I wrote up my field notes at the end of the day. The realisation of these themes emerging from the research were ways of organising the volume of information I was receiving.

When I had finished the period of field research, I went about analysing the notes, interviews, and documents in the following way. First, I read the fieldnotes, notes, and transcripts I had made and identified themes and sub-themes. Second, I sorted and coded the themes into categories and sub-categories and incorporated relevant literature into my coding. At the end of this process I had organised the material for interpretation. Authors typically propose similar methods to reduce raw description for interpretation. Reduction goes by various names, analytic induction (Denzin, 1989b), constant comparative method (Glaser and Strauss, 1967), processing the data (Lincoln and Guba, 1985). In writing-up the text I based my interpretations on the written documents I produced in the research. In producing a text I was guided by a descriptive realist style that attempted to allow the world being interpreted to speak for itself (Denzin, 1989a). Descriptive realism reveals the conflictual, contradictory nature of lived experience and realises that no single interpretation can completely capture problematic events.

Interpretive interactionism tries to bring lived experience before the reader (Denzin, 1989a). Central to the development of such an interpretation is the use of thick description (Geertz, 1973) to interpret and capture the meanings persons bring to their experiences (Denzin, 1989b). Thick description allows the reader to understand the interpretation of child welfare work. What I have told and interpreted was what I saw and understood. Another person, an American, a woman, a minority person, a Native American would see differently and tell the story differently. Just as my own biography framed the question so has it framed the interpretation. It must always be thus.

References

Addams, J. (1910/1981). *Twenty years at Hull House*, Signet: New York.

Agger, B. (1991). *A critical theory of public life: Knowledge, discourse and politics in an age of decline*, Falmer: Bristol, PA.

Anderson, J. (1990). 'Changing needs, challenging children', in *The Adoption Assistance Act and Child Welfare Act of 1980: The first ten years*, The North American Council on Adoptable Children: St Paul, MN, pp. 41-49.

Anderson, P. G. (1989). The origin, emergence, and professional recognition of child protection. *Social Service Review*, Vol. 63, pp. 222-244.

Arches, J. (1985). Don't burn, organize: A structural analysis of burnout in the human services. *Catalyst*, Vol. 5, No. 17/18, pp. 15-20.

Arendt, H. (1958). *The human condition*, University of Chicago Press: Chicago.

Atkinson, P. (1988). Ethnomethodology: A critical review. *Annual Review of Sociology*, Vol. 14, pp. 441-465.

Baily, T. F. and Baily, W. H. (1983). *Child welfare practice*, Jossey-Bass: San Francisco.

Baldacci, L. (1992, April 13). Judge cracks down on no-shows. *Chicago Sun-Times*, p. 44.

Barrett, M. C. and McKelvey, J. (1980). Stresses and strains on the child care worker: Typologies for assessment. *Child Welfare*, Vol. 59, pp. 277-285.

Bartlett, H. M. (1970). *The common base of social work practice*, National Association of Social Workers: Washington, DC.

Best, L. (1990). *Threatened children: Rhetoric and concern about child-victims*, University of Chicago Press: Chicago.

Blumer, H. (1986). *Symbolic interactionism*, University of California Press: Berkeley, CA.

Blyth, E. and Milner, J. (1990). The process of inter-agency work, in The Violence against Children Study Group, *Taking child abuse seriously*, Unwin Hyman: London, pp. 194-211.

Bogdan, R. C. and Biklen, S. K. (1982). *Qualitative research for education: An introduction to theory and methods*, Allyn and Bacon: Boston, MA.

Born, C. E. (1983). Proprietary firms and child welfare services: Patterns and implications. *Child Welfare*, Vol. 62, pp. 109-118.

Bureau of the Census. (1991). *Census of population and housing, 1990: Summary Tape File 1A. Extract on CD-ROM (Illinois)* (Machine-readable data file), Washington, DC.

Burghardt, S. (1986). 'Marxist theory and social work', in Turner, F. J. (ed.), *Social work treatment: Interlocking theoretical approaches* (3rd ed.), Free Press: New York, pp. 590-617.

Cardenal, R. S. (1991). 'Alone and very scared', in Nabokov, P. (ed.), *Native American testimony*, New York: Viking, pp. 413-418.

Chau, K. L. (1989). 'Sociocultural dissonance among ethnic minority populations,' *Social Casework*, Vol. 70, pp. 224-230.

Clifford, J. and Marcus, G. E. (1986). *Writing culture*, University of California Press: Berkeley, CA.

Copeland, M. (1991, December 13). 'Tot's death triggers probe of DCFS.' *Chicago Tribune*, Section 2, p. 6.

Corby, B. (1987). *Working with child abuse*, Open University Press: Milton Keynes, UK.

Corrections. (1991, July 18). *Chicago Tribune*, Section 1, p. 3.

Costin, L. (1985). 'The historical context of child welfare,' in Laird, J. and Hartman, A. (eds.), *A handbook of child welfare: Context, knowledge, and practice*, Free Press: New York, pp. 34-60.

Costin, L. B., Bell, C. J. and Downs, S. W. (1991). *Child welfare: Policies and practice* (4th ed.), Longman: New York.

Crystal, D. (1989). 'Asian Americans and the myth of the model minority,' *Social Casework*, Vol. 70, pp. 405-413.

Cuadros, P. F. (1991). 'Experts' report finds DCFS is a dysfunctional family unable to care for its children,' *The Illinois Brief*, Vol. 48, No. 1, pp. 1,3.

Cummings, J. (1992, March 31). 'Meanwhile, back at the coalface . . .,' *The Bulletin*, pp. 42-44.

Denzin, N. K. (1987). *The alcoholic self*, Sage: Newbury Park, CA.

Denzin, N. K. (1989a). *Interpretive interactionism*, Sage: Newbury Park, CA..

Denzin, N. K. (1989b). *The research act*, Prentice Hall: Englewood Cliffs, NJ.

Denzin, N. K. (1992). *Symbolic interactionism and cultural studies: The politics of interpretation*, Blackwell: Cambridge, MA.

Dingwall, R., Eekelaar, J. and Murray, T. (1983). *The protection of children*, Blackwell: Oxford, UK.

Donzelot, J. (1979). *The policing of families*, Pantheon: New York.

DuBray, W. (1991). 'The role of social work education for Indian child welfare,' in Wares, D. (ed.), *Developing linkages for the future: Indian child welfare and schools of social work*, Norman, OK: University of Oklahoma School of Social Work and Three Feathers Associates, pp. 38-49.

Dugger, C. W. (1992, September 9). 'Fatal beating points up a system in crisis,' *The New York Times*, pp. A1, C19.

Edwards, J. (1987). 'Why the public don't like social workers,' in Department of Social Policy and Social Science, Royal Holloway and Bedford New College, *After Beckford?* (Social Policy Papers No. 1), Egham, Surrey, UK, pp. 131-136.

Eisner, E. W. (1991). *The enlightened eye*. New York: Macmillan.

Esposito, G. and Fine, M. (1985). 'The field of child welfare as a world of work,' in J. Laird and A. Hartman (eds.), *A handbook of child welfare: Context, knowledge and practic*, New York: The Free Press, pp. 727-740.

Faller, K. C. (ed.). (1981). *Social work with abused and neglected children*. New York: Free Press.

Fanshel. D. (1980). 'The future of social work research, ' in D. Fanshel (ed.), *Future of social work research*, Washington, DC: National Association of Social Workers, pp. 3-18.

Feyerabend, P. (1975). *Against method*. London: New Left Books.

Findlay, P. C. (1978). 'Critical theory and social work practice,' *Catalyst*, Vol. 1, No. 3, pp. 53-68.

Foucault, M. (1979). *Discipline and punish*. New York: Vintage.

Foucault, M. (1980). *Power/knowledge*. New York: Pantheon.

Fraser, N. (1989). *Unruly practices*. Minneapolis: University of Minnesota Press.

Freire, P. (1970). *Pedagogy of the oppressed*. New York: Seabury.

Freire, P. (1985). *The politics of education*. Granby, MA: Bergin and Garvey.

Frost, N. and Stein, M. (1989). *The politics of child welfare*. Hemel Hempstead, UK: Harvester Wheatsheaf.

Fryer, G. E., Miyoshi, T. J. and Thomas, P. J. (1989). 'The relationship of child protection worker attitudes to attrition from the field,' *Child Abuse and Neglect*, Vol. 13, pp. 345-350.

Fryer, G.E., Poland, J.E., Bross, D.C. and Krugman, R.D. (1988). 'The child protective service worker: A profile of needs, attitudes, and utilization of professional resources,' *Child Abuse and Neglect*, Vol. 12, pp. 481-490.

Garfinkel. H. (1967). *Studies in ethnomethodology*. Englewood Cliffs, NJ: Prentice-Hall.

Garfinkel, H. and Sacks, H. (1970/1990). 'On formal structures of practical actions,' in J. Coulter (ed.), *Ethnomethodological sociology*, Brookfield, VT: Edward Elgar, pp. 55-84.

Geertz, C. (1973). *The interpretation of cultures*. New York: Basic Books.

Geertz, C. (1976). "From the native's point of view": On the nature of anthropological understanding,' in K. H. Basso and H. A. Selby (eds.), *Meaning in anthropology*, Albuquerque: University of New Mexico Press, pp. 221-237.

Geiser, R. L. (1973). *The illusion of caring: Children in foster care*. Boston, MA: Beacon.

Gelles, R. (1975). 'The social construction of child abuse,' *American Journal of Orthopsychiatry*, Vol. 45, pp. 363-371.

Gelles, R. J. (1983). 'Foreword,' in R. Dingwall, J. Eekelaar, and T. Murray. *The protection of children*, Oxford, UK: Blackwell, pp. vii-viii.

Germain, C. B. and Gitterman, A. (1980). *The life model of social work practice*. New York: Columbia University Press.

Gil, D. G. (1985). 'The ideological context of child welfare, ' in J. Laird and A. Hartman (eds.), *A handbook of child welfare: Context, knowledge, and practice*, New York: Free Press, pp. 11-33.

Gillespie, B. (1985). 'Because I care,' in Illinois Department of Children and Family Services, *Child welfare services practice handbook*. Springfield, IL.

Giovannoni, J. M. and Becerra, R. M. (1979). *Defining child abuse*. New York: Free Press.

Glaser, B. G. and Strauss, A. L. (1967). *The discovery of grounded theory*. Chicago: Aldine.

Gliatto, T., Huzinec, M., Lynn, A., and Johnson, K. (1992, September 7), 'The war in the trenches,' *People Weekly*, pp. 55-56.

Gold, R. (1958). 'Roles in sociological field observations,' *Social Forces*, Vol. 36, pp. 217-223.

Gordon, L. (1985). 'Child abuse, gender, and the myth of family independence: A historical critique,' *Child Welfare*, Vol. 64, pp. 213-224.

Gordon, L. (1988). *Heroes of their own lives: The politics and history of family violence*. New York: Viking.

Goroff, N. N. (1978). 'Conflict theories and social work education, *Journal of Sociology and Social Welfare*, Vol. 5, pp. 498-507.

Gould, K. (1988). 'Asian and Pacific Islanders: Myth and reality, '*Social Work*, Vol. 33, pp. 142-148.

Greene, B. (1990, July 29). 'Finally, a victory for Sarah,' *Chicago Tribune*, Section 5, p. 1.

Greene. B. (1991, February 24). 'Something just seems wrong,' *Chicago Tribune*, Section 5, pp. 1, 6.

Gullerud, E. N. and McMahon, A. (1992, July). 'Columbus in retrospect: Decolonizing Native American Child Welfare,' paper presented at the 7th Biennial Conference of The InterUniversity Consortium on International Social Development, Washington, DC.

Habermas, J. (1979). *Communication and the evolution of society*. Boston: Beacon.

Hardin, M. (1990). 'Ten years later: Implementation of Public Law 96-272 by the courts,' in The North American Council on Adoptable Children, *The Adoption Assistance Act and Child Welfare Act of 1980: The first ten years*, St Paul, MN, pp. 51-74.

Hartman, A. (1990). Children in a careless society. *Social Work*, Vol. 35, pp. 483-484.

Hartman, A. (1991). Social worker-in-situation. *Social Work*, Vol. 36, pp. 195-196.

Hasenfeld, Y. (1972). 'People processing organizations: An exchange approach,' *American Sociological Review*, Vol. 37, pp. 256-263.

Hauswald, L. (1987). 'External pressure/internal change: Child neglect on the Navajo reservation,' in N. Scheper-Hughes (Ed.), *Child Survival*, Dordrecht, Holland: Reidel, pp. 145-164.

Hegar, R. L. and Hunzeker, J. M. (1988). 'Moving toward empowerment-based practice in public child welfare,' *Social Work*, Vol. 33, pp. 499-502.

Hirayama, H. and Cetingok, M. (1988). 'Empowerment: A social work approach for Asian immigrants,' *Social Casework*, Vol. 69, pp. 41-47.

Hogan, P. T. and Siu, S-F. (1988). 'Minority children and the child welfare system: An historical perspective,' *Social Work*, Vol. 33, pp. 493-497.

Horkheimer, M. (1989). *Critical theory*. New York: Continuum.

Hughes, D.M. (1987). 'When cultural rights conflict with the 'best interests of the child : A view from inside the child welfare system,' in N. Scheper-Hughes (ed.), *Child Survival*, Dordrecht, Holland: Reidel, pp. 377-382.

Hutchison, E. (1990). 'Child maltreatment: Can it be defined?' *Social Service Review*, Vol. 64, pp. 61-78.

Hutchison, E.D. (1992). 'Child welfare as a woman's issue,' *Families in Society*, Vol. 73, pp. 67-77.

Illinois Department of Children and Family Services. (1986). *Care enough to call*. Springfield, IL.

Illinois Department of Children and Family Services. (1989). *Helping children, saving families*. Springfield, IL.

Illinois Department of Children and Family Services. (1992). *Community meetings series, March-April 1992*. Springfield, IL.

Illinois Legislative Investigating Commission. (1983). *The child victim: A report to the General Assembly*. Chicago.

Imre, R. W. (1991). 'What do we need to know for good practice?' *Social Work*, Vol. 36, pp. 198-200.

Indian Child Welfare Act of 1978, 25 U. S. C. §§ 1901-1963 (1978).

Jacobs, G. (1970). 'Life in the colonies: Welfare workers and clients', in G. Jacobs (ed.), *The participant observer*, New York: George Braziller, pp. 246-259.

James, G. (1979). 'The child-centred approach to children in care', in D. Brandon and B. Jordan (eds.), *Creative social work* Oxford, UK: Basil Blackwell, pp. 61-68.

Jansen, G. G. (1992). 'Helping perspectives of South East Asian refugee women as paraprofessional helpers', unpublished doctoral thesis, University of Illinois at Urbana-Champaign.

Jayaratne, S. and Chess, W. A. (1984). 'Job satisfaction, burnout, and turnover: A national study', *Social Work*, Vol. 29, pp. 448-453.

Jenkins, S. and Norman, E. (1975). *Beyond placement: Mothers view foster care.* New York: Columbia University Press.

Jimenez, M. A. (1990). 'Permanency planning and the Child Abuse Prevention and Treatment Act: The paradox of child welfare policy', *Journal of Sociology and Social Welfare*, Vol. 17, pp. 55-72.

Johnson, J. M. (1975). *Doing field research.* New York: Free Press.

Johnston, P. (1981). 'Indigenous children at risk', *Policy Options/Options Politiques*, Vol. 1, No. 2, pp. 47-50.

Kadushin, A. (1980). *Child welfare services* (3rd ed.). New York: Macmillan.

Kadushin, A. (1987). 'Child welfare services', in A. Minahan (ed.), *Encyclopedia of Social Work* (18th Ed,)), Silver Spring, MD: National Association of Social Workers, pp. 265-275.

Kagle, J.D. (1984). *Social work records.* Homewood, IL: Dorsey.

Kamerman, S. B. and Kahn, A. J. (1990). 'If CPS is driving child welfare – where do we go from here?' *Public Welfare*, Vol. 48, No. 1, pp. 9-13, 46.

Kantrowitz, B., McCormick, J. and Wingert, P. (1991, May 31). 'Children lost in the quagmire', *Newsweek*, p. 64.

Karger, H. (1981). 'Burnout as alienation', *Social Service Review*, Vol. 55, pp. 271-283.

Karwath, R. (1991a, October 30). 'Months after kids' deaths, DCFS worker reports they're fine,' *Chicago Tribune*, Section 1, p. 1.

Karwath, R. (1991b, September 3). 'DCFS struggles to be a better parent', *Chicago Tribune*, Section 2, p. 6.

Karwath, R. (1991c, October 6). '"Sarah" case judge will need wisdom of Solomon to rule', *Chicago Tribune*, Section 2, p. 1.

Kass, J. (1988, May 6). 'Suspect had fear of conspiracies', *Chicago Tribune*, Section, p. 1.

Kellner, D. (1989). *Critical Theory, marxism and modernity.* Baltimore, MD: John Hopkins University Press.

Kempe, R. S. and Kempe, C. H. (1978). *Child abuse.* Cambridge, MA: Harvard University Press.

Kempe, C.H., Silverman, F.N., Steele, B.T., Droegemueller, W. and Silver, H.K. (1962/1985). 'The battered-child syndrome', *Child Abuse and Neglect*, Vol. 9, pp. 143-154.

Kinard, E.M. (1987). 'Child abuse and neglect', in A. Minahan (ed.), *Encyclopedia of Social Work* (18th Ed.). Silver Spring, MD: National Association of Social Workers, pp. 223-231.

Korbin, J. (1977). 'Anthropological contributions to the study of child abuse', *Child Abuse and Neglect*, Vol. 1, pp. 7-24.

Korbin, J. (1979). 'A cross-cultural perspective on the role of the community in child abuse and neglect', *Child Abuse and Neglect*, Vol 3, pp. 9-18.

Korbin, J. (1980). 'The cultural context of abuse and neglect', *Child Abuse and Neglect*, Vol. 4, pp. 3-13.

Lancaster, J. B. and Gelles, R. J. (1987). 'Introduction', in R. J. Gelles and J. B. Lancaster (Eds.), *Child abuse and neglect*, New York: Aldine De Gruyter, pp. 3-12.

Lasch, C. (1977). *Haven in a heartless world: The family besieged.* New York: Basic Books.

Lasch, C. (1979). *The culture of narcissism.* New York: Warner

Leonard, P. (1984). *Personality and ideology: towards a materialist understanding of the individual.* London: Macmillan.

Levitt, S., Mills, B. K., and Freedman, A. (1992, September 7). 'Not scared, not silent', *People Weekly*, pp. 48-49.

Lieberman, A. A., Hornby, H. and Russell, M. (1988). 'Analyzing the educational backgrounds and work experiences of child welfare personnel: A national study', *Social Work*, Vol. 33, pp. 485-489.

Lincoln, Y. S. and Guba, E. G. (1985). *Naturalistic inquiry.* Newbury Park, CA: Sage.

Lubove, R. (1969). *The professional altruist.* New York: Atheneum.

Lujuan, C., DeBruyn, L. M., May, P. A. and Bird, M. E. (1989). 'Profile of abused and neglected American Indian children in the Southwest', *Child Abuse and Neglect*, Vol. 13, pp. 449-461.

Lum, D. (1982). 'Toward a framework for social work practice with minorities', *Social Work*, Vol. 27, pp. 244-249.

Marcus, G. E. and Fischer, M. M. J. (1986). *Anthropology as cultural critique.* Chicago: University of Chicago Press.

Massat, C. R. (1992). 'Lifting the shadow: An analysis of demographic characteristics of maltreating parents and heads of households with children in care', unpublished doctoral thesis, University of Illinois at Urbana-Champaign.

Matthiessen, P. (1991). *In the spirit of Crazy Horse.* New York: Viking.

Maynard, D. W. (1984). *Inside plea bargaining.* New York: Plenum.

McMahon, A. (1990). 'Social work and Aborigines', *Australian Social Work*, Vol. 43, No. 3, pp. 11-14.

McMahon, A. and Allen-Meares, P. (1992). 'Is social work racist? A content analysis of recent literature', *Social Work*, Vol. 37, pp. 533-539.

McMahon, A. and Gullerud, E. N. (1995). 'Native American agencies for Native American children: Fulfilling the promise of the Indian Child Welfare Act', *Journal of Sociology and Social Welfare*, Vol. 22, pp. 87-98.

McMahon, A. and Kogolo, A. (1988). 'Living a new way: a case-study in community self-management', in B. Harvey and S. McGinty (Eds.), *Learning My Way, Papers from the National Conference on Adult Aboriginal Learning*, Mt Lawley, Western Australia: Institute of Applied Aboriginal Studies, pp. 148 -153.

Mills, C. W. (1959). *The sociological imagination*. New York: Oxford University Press.

Mishler, E. G. (1986). *Research interviewing*. Cambridge, MA: Harvard University Press.

Mokuau, N. (1990). 'A family-centered approach in native Hawaiian culture. *Families in Society*, Vol. 71. pp. 607-613.

Montiel, M. and Wong, P. (1983). A theoretical critique of the minority perspective', *Social Casework*, 64, 112-117.

National Indian Policy Center. (1992). *Report to Congress*. Washington, DC: George Washington University.

Parton, N. (1985). *The politics of child abuse*. London: Macmillan.

Parton, N. (1990). 'Taking child abuse seriously', in The Violence against Children Study Group (ed.), *Taking child abuse seriously*, London: Unwin Hyman, pp. 7-24.

Patton, M. Q. (1980). *Qualitative evaluation methods*. Beverly Hills: Sage.

Pecora, P. J., Briar, K. H., and Zlotnick, J. L. (1989). *Addressing the program and personnel crisis in child welfare*. Silver Spring, MD: National Association of Social Workers.

Pelton, L. H. (Ed.) (1981). *The social context of child abuse and neglect*. New York: Human Sciences Press.

Pelton, L. H. (1989). *For reasons of poverty*. New York: Praeger.

Pelton, L. H. (1990). 'Resolving the crisis in child welfare', *Public Welfare*, Vol. 48, No. 4, pp. 19-25, 45.

Pelton, L. H. (1991). 'Beyond permanency planning: Restructuring the public child welfare system', *Social Work*, Vol. 36, pp. 337-343.

Piasecki, J. M., Manson, S. M., Biernoff, M. P., Hiat, A. B., Taylor, S. S. and Bechtold, D. W. (1989). 'Abuse and neglect of American Indian children: Findings from a survey of federal providers', *American Indian and Alaska Native Mental Health Research*, Vol. 3, No. 2, pp. 43-62.

Pithouse, A. (1987). *Social Work: The social organisation of an invisible trade*. Aldershot, UK: Avebury.

Piven, F. F. and Cloward, R. A. (1971). *Regulating the poor: The functions of public welfare*. New York: Random House.

Plantz, M. C., Hubbell, R. Barrett, B. J. and Dobrec, A. (1988). *Indian Child Welfare: A status report* (Contract No. 105-82-1602). Washington, DC:

Administration for Children, Youth and Families and Bureau of Indian Affairs.

Pollner, M. (1987). *Mundane reason*. Cambridge, UK: Cambridge University Press.

Press, A. (1992, August 10). 'Old too soon, wise too late?' *Newsweek*, pp. 22-24.

Rein, M. and White, S. H. (1981). 'Knowledge for practice', *Social Service Review*, Vol. 55, pp. 1-41.

Richards, K. (1992). *Tender mercies: Inside the world of a child abuse investigator*. Chicago, IL: Noble Press.

Rubin, L. B. (1981). 'Sociological research: The subjective dimension', *Symbolic Interactionism*, Vol. 4, No. 1, pp. 42-57.

Ryan, R.A. (1980). 'A community perspective for mental health research', *Social Casework*, Vol. 61, pp. 507-511.

Samantrai, K. (1991). 'Clinical social work in public child welfare practice', *Social Work*, Vol. 36, pp. 359-366.

Samantrai, K. (1992). 'Factors in the decision to leave: Retaining social workers with MSWs in public child welfare', *Social Work*, Vol. 37, pp. 454-458.

Sands, R. G. (1990). 'Ethnographic research: A qualitative research approach to study the interdisciplinary team', *Social Work in Health Care*, Vol. 15, pp. 115-129.

Sarri, R. and Finn, J. (1992). 'Child welfare policy and practice: Rethinking the history of our certainties', *Children and Youth Services Review*, Vol. 14, pp. 219-236.

Satyamurti, C. (1981). *Occupational survival: The case of the local authority social worker*. Oxford, UK: Blackwell.

Scott, D. (1990). 'Practice wisdom: The neglected source of practice research,' *Social Work*, Vol. 35, pp. 564-568.

Seabury, B. (1985). 'The beginning phase: Engagement, initial assessment, and contracting', in J. Laird and A. Hartman (eds.), *A handbook of child welfare: Context, knowledge and practice*, New York: The Free Press, pp. 335-359.

Silverman, D. (1985). *Qualitative methodology and sociology*. Aldershot, UK: Gower.

Silverman, D. (1992, July 25). 'Sniper ends girl's dream to flee Riverside', *Chicago Tribune*, pp. 1, 6.

Siu, S-F. and Hogan, P. T. (1989a). 'Public child welfare: The need for clinical social work', *Social Work*, Vol. 34, pp. 423-428.

Siu, S-F. and Hogan, P. T. (1989b). 'Common clinical themes in child welfare', *Social Work*, Vol. 34, pp. 339-345.

Spradley, J. P. (1980). *Participant observation*. New York: Holt, Rinehart and Winston.

Stehno, S.M. (1990). 'The elusive continuum of child welfare services: Implications for minority children and youths', *Child Welfare*, Vol. 69, pp. 551-562.

Stein, T. J. (1987). 'Foster care for children', in A. Minahan (ed.), *Encyclopedia of Social Work* (18th Ed.). Silver Spring, MD: National Association of Social Workers, pp. 639-650.

Steinberg, N. (1991, August 22). 'Boy, 11, killed by gang gunfire ...', *Chicago Sun-Times*, p. 24.

Street, A. F. (1992). *Inside nursing: A critical ethnography of clinical nursing practice.* Albany, NY: State University of New York Press.

Sundel, M. and Homan, C. C. (1979). 'Prevention in child welfare: A framework for management and practice', *Child Welfare*, Vol. 58, pp. 510-521.

Thomas, J. (1983). 'Toward a critical ethnography', *Urban Life*, Vol. 11, pp. 477-490.

Tomlinson, J. (1985). 'The history of Aboriginal community work', in R. Thorpe and J. Petruchenia (eds.), *Community work or social change?: An Australian perspective*, London: Routledge and Kegan Paul, pp. 144-163.

Trattner, W. I. (1984). *From poor law to welfare state.* New York: The Free Press.

Ulmer, G. (1989). *Teletheory.* New York: Routledge.

Unger, S. (ed.). (1977). *The destruction of American Indian families.* New York: Association on American Indian Affairs.

US Department of Health and Human Services. (1988). *Study findings: Study of national incidence and prevalence of child abuse and neglect: 1988* (Contract No. 105-85-1702). Washington, DC.

van Manen, M. (1990). *Researching lived experience.* New York: State University of New York.

Wattenberg, E. (1985). 'In a different light: A feminist perspective on the role of mothers in father-daughter incest', *Child Welfare*, Vol. 64, pp. 203-211.

Weick. A. (1992). 'Building a strengths perspective for social work', in D. Saleeby (ed.), *The strengths perspective in social work practice*, New York: Longman, pp. 18-26.

White, R. B. and Cornely, D. A. (1981). 'Navajo child abuse and neglect study: A comparison group examination of abuse and neglect of Navajo children', *Child Abuse and Neglect*, Vol. 5, pp. 9-17.

Wichlacz, C. R., Lane, J. M. and Kempe, C. H. (1978). 'Indian Child Welfare: A community team approach to protective services', *Child Abuse and Neglect*, Vol. 2, pp. 29-35.

Wilensky, H. L. and Lebeaux, C. N. (1965). *Industrial society and social welfare.* New York: Free Press.

Wills, C. (1992, August 7). 'Child welfare agency facing crisis situation, say experts', *Champaign-Urbana News-Gazette*, pp. A-1, A-10.

Witkin, S. L. and Gottschalk, S. (1988). 'Alternative criteria for theory evaluation', *Social Service Review*, Vol. 62, pp. 211-224.

Wood, K. M. (1978). 'Casework effectiveness: A new look at the research evidence', *Social Work*, Vol. 23, pp. 437-458.

Young, I. M. (1990). *Justice and the politics of difference*. Princeton, NJ: Princeton University Press.

Zimmerman, D. H. (1969). 'Record-keeping and the intake process in a public welfare agency', in S. Wheeler (ed.), *On record: Files and dossiers in American life*, New York: Russell Sage Foundation, pp. 319-354.